Operation Inasmuch

OTHER LAKE HICKORY RESOURCES

James H. Royston, Executive Editor
George W. Bullard Jr., Senior Editor
SeniorEditor@LakeHickoryResources.org

Spiritual Leadership in a Secular Age
Building Bridges Instead of Barriers
by Edward H. Hammett

Seeds for the Future
Growing Organic Leaders for Living Churches
by Robert D. Dale

Pursuing the Full Kingdom Potential of Your Congregation
by George W. Bullard Jr.

---

www.lakehickoryresources.com

Operation Inasmuch

*Mobilizing Believers
beyond the Walls of the Church*

DAVID W. CROCKER

Lake Hickory RESOURCES
ST. LOUIS, MISSOURI

Cover art: Getty Images
Cover and interior design: Elizabeth Wright

See more Lake Hickory Resources at
www.lakehickoryresources.com.

10 9 8 7 6 5 4 3 2 1   05 06 07 08 09

Library of Congress Cataloging-in-Publication Data
Crocker, David W.
  Operation Inasmuch : mobilizing believers beyond the walls of the church / David W. Crocker.
      p. cm.
  "'Truly, I say to you, inasmuch as you did it to one of the least of these my brethren, you did it to me' Matthew 25:40."
  ISBN 10: 0-827227-21-3 (pbk. : alk. paper)
  ISBN 13: 978-0-827227-21-7
  1. Operation Inasmuch. 2. City missions. 3. Evangelistic work. I. Title.
  BV2653.C76 2005
  269'.2—dc22

                                                            2005004525

Printed in the United States of America

Contents

112013

This book is dedicated to

the congregation of Snyder Memorial Baptist Church
Fayetteville, North Carolina,

for their willingness to follow the vision of getting outside the
walls of their church house to minister to the poor and
marginalized of their community,

and their support in efforts to share this vision with any and
all congregational leaders who want to do the same;

and

to my life and ministry partner, Clara,
without whose patience and complete support
this vision might never have materialized.

EDITORS' FOREWORD

Inspiration and Wisdom for Twenty-first–Century Christian Leaders

You have chosen wisely in deciding to study and learn from a **Lake Hickory Resources** book. Lake Hickory Resources publishes for

- congregational leaders who desire to serve effectively
- Christian ministers who pursue excellence in service
- members of a congregation that desires to reach its full Kingdom potential
- denominational leaders who want to come alongside affiliated congregations in a servant leadership role

Lake Hickory Resources is an inspiration and wisdom sharing vehicle of Lake Hickory Learning Communities.* LHLC is the web of relationships developing from the base of Hollifield Leadership Center [www.Hollifield.org] near Hickory, North Carolina. LHLC addresses emerging strategic issues of leadership development for congregations, denominations, and parachurch organizations.

The mission of **Lake Hickory Resources** is currently being expressed through two meaningful avenues. First, George Bullard, executive coach for Lake Hickory Learning Communities, also is senior editor for *Net Results* magazine [www.NetResults.org], a national, trans-denominational publication that appears monthly in either print or electronic form.

---

*Lake Hickory Learning Communities is a ministry of www.NorthCarolinaBaptists.org.

Second, **Lake Hickory Resources** publishes books in partnership with the Christian Board of Publication. Once this partnership is in full production it will produce eight to twelve new books each year.

We welcome your comments on these books, and we welcome your suggestions for new subject areas and authors we ought to consider.

James H. Royston, Executive Editor
George W. Bullard Jr., Senior Editor
SeniorEditor@LakeHickoryResources.org

Welcome to the Adventure

The Christian life is an adventure, or, at least that's what it is supposed to be. Even a casual reading of the Gospels reveals that. In purchasing and reading this book, you are about to discover an adventuresome expression of the Christian life for yourself and your church.

This book is the latest in a series of steps taken to share the vision of Operation Inasmuch. It began with the place of its origination—Snyder Memorial Baptist Church, Fayetteville, North Carolina, when I was pastor there in 1995. As soon as it was suggested that we could share our experience with others, that congregation responded eagerly. They gave me time away from my pastoral responsibilities to write a manual that would tell the Operation Inasmuch story and instruct other congregational leaders in conducting their own one-day, hands-on blitz of their own community. Ten years later, the good folk of Snyder Memorial are continuing this vital and contagious ministry.

I am indebted to George Bullard, former director of the Hollifield Leadership Center and Lake Hickory Learning Communities and personal friend, for publishing the initial Operation Inasmuch manual. It has exceeded our expectations in aiding churches that want to make a difference in their communities. As of this writing, Operation Inasmuch is done by churches in eight states. The total number of Operation Inasmuch churches is in excess of four hundred and growing.

With the establishment of Lake Hickory Resources, a new publication imprint under Christian Board of Publication, greater access than ever is being made possible for this book. George Bullard deserves the credit for this move as well.

As you read this book, you will discover ways you can help more people and more effectively demonstrate God's compassion for those who need it most, as well as facilitate real spiritual growth for the members of your church. After you have conducted your own Operation Inasmuch, log onto our Web site—www.operationinasmuch.com—and let us know of your experience.

May God guide you on the adventure of Operation Inasmuch.

David W. Crocker
October 2004

1

Circulating the Saints

Every problem that the country faces is being solved in some community by some group or some individual. The question is how to get connected so that the whole nation can solve problems.

PRESIDENT GEORGE H. W. BUSH

During the reign of Oliver Cromwell in England in the nineteenth century, the British government ran low on silver coins. Lord Cromwell sent out envoys into the country in search of silver. They found some in the cathedrals of the land. They reported back to Cromwell, "The only silver we could find was the statues of the saints standing in the churches." He replied, "Good. We'll melt down the saints and put them into circulation."[1]

Would that it were that easy—melting down believers and circulating them like coinage in the world. This is a good image of getting the church into the world, but that is all. It is only an image. Many a congregational leader, both professional and lay,

1

struggles with the implementation of that portion of the church's mission to scatter into the community, to be the church while *disbursed* in the world as much as when *gathered* inside the walls of their buildings. Not many persevere in this struggle. Some give up and leave the church. Others give in to the demands of a maintenance ministry, choosing to survive rather than take the risks necessary to break free from the bonds of institutionalism. Only a few have what it takes to lead their congregations outside the walls of their buildings, and when they do, they find the going hard.

This dilemma is the subject of Edward Hammett's book *The Gathered and Scattered Church* (1999). He says powerful forces are at work to keep today's church from being scattered into their community:

- Most Christians believe the purpose of the church is to gather together, maintain ecclesiastical programs, and serve persons in the congregation. Thus, Christians spend most of their time looking inward and taking care of their own.
- Most convictions about the nature of the church are not grounded in Scripture but in the traditions of friends, ancestors, and/or family members.
- It is easier to maintain ecclesiastical machinery such as church programs, committees, and social agendas than it is to be a people on mission in the world.
- Traditional standards of success for a church are guided by the wrong concepts of what it means to be the people of God. Most churches and their staff and leaders are evaluated on how many people participate in church programs rather than on how many go from the church and make a difference in the world.
- The inward focus of most churches has created apathy. Committed Christians have given up on their dream of making a difference, and therefore have fallen into the trap of building and maintaining the ecclesiastical machinery.[2]

Encountering these realities almost on a daily basis has discouraged many congregational leaders. They believe that a new church, one without confining traditions, is required if we are to make much difference in the community. However, some leaders *are* still asking questions that will not allow them to surrender just yet to the bondage of institutionalism as represented in the church depicted by the above statements: "What if we could mobilize significant numbers of our congregation to go out into the community and minister to the hurts and hopes of our neighbors?"

"What if we could do something to help our members discover that their skills and experiences are valuable tools of ministry?"

"What if there was some way to appeal to the values of younger believers in such a way as to see them actually get involved in ministry?

"What if there was a way to help our community see the church as a vital, contributory, authentic Christian witness in the community?"

This book is offered for the congregational leaders who live with these and other questions like them. In this book we will tell the story of Operation Inasmuch, an effective plan for mobilizing believers to scatter into their community and to minister to some of the hurts and hopes of their neighbors. As they do this, church members discover their value to the Kingdom and improve the church's image in the community. Operation Inasmuch offers a proven way for the church, any church, to get outside the walls of their buildings and be the body of Christ—the hands, feet, and voice of Christ—in the world. If you are a congregational leader who still believes it is not only possible but necessary to circulate the saints into the world, read on.

What Is Operation Inasmuch?

Operation Inasmuch is a one-day mission blitz by church folk in their community. It is an intergenerational event (and in some cases an interracial and interdenominational event) mobilizing Christians to heal some of the hurts of a neighborhood or an entire community. Operation Inasmuch is

- a day devoted to helping people at their points of need
- reaching out to strangers in Christian love and understanding
- fostering racial harmony through working together
- a surge in spiritual growth
- acknowledging the mission field in one's own backyard
- accepting the Great Commission
- strengthening Christian fellowship
- discovering how one's personal gifts can be used in mission work

More to the point, Operation Inasmuch is Christians doing the work of the church instead of church work. The distinction is significant. Church work is what we do to keep the institution percolating. It is committee work, planning, prayer meetings, budget work, and so on. The work of the church, however, is going outside the walls of the church buildings to apply God's love to human hurts and hopes wherever they are found.

This in no way denigrates church work. As a pastor, I understand the necessity of maintaining the home base, and I appreciate the hundreds of hours that dedicated people invest in these vital activities each year. But I also know how consuming those activities can become. We do not intend for this to happen, but it does. Institutionalism can be an insidious drain on a church's vitality. Operation Inasmuch is one way dozens of churches have found to break free of the inertia of institutionalism and get involved again in the work of the church. Let me put it this way: Operation Inasmuch is

- a city attorney delivering lunches for volunteers all over town
- a retired Army officer roofing the house of a family he has never met

- a school teacher cleaning a shut-in's yard
- a secretary sewing lap robes for nursing home patients and blankets for homeless persons
- a young soldier splitting and delivering firewood to people who depend on wood as their primary source of heat
- a thirteen-year-old girl mouthing the words to a story about Jesus for a puppet in a backyard Bible club in a neighborhood where children have never seen such a thing
- a couple—a businessman and a school counselor—visiting the people whose homes are being repaired, praying with them, and making sure they understand why strangers are working on their home
- a mother of three making "Life Books" for children in foster care (Life Books are notebooks containing pictures and other memories of their childhood as they move from family to family)
- third-grade children planting flowers
- a real estate developer and community college administrator building a wheelchair ramp for an elderly man who has not been out of his house for a year because he could not negotiate the steps
- a high school sophomore cleaning off years of grime and covering weathering with a fresh coat of paint on the home of a widow who cannot afford to pay a professional painter to do the job
- a group of fifth grade boys placing door hangers advertising the church's contemporary worship service on three hundred apartments.

Coming of Age

The phone rang one more time in an otherwise routine day filled with drop-in visits, meetings with staff, sermon preparation, and so on. But this call proved unique. The caller was the secretary of the local city manager, Roger Stancil. Since Roger is an active member of the church I served as pastor, it wasn't all that unusual to hear from his office. He frequently called to ask about church work, issue a request for an invocation at the city council meeting, or inquire about some such thing. This was a request all right, just nothing I had heard before. The secretary asked if Roger could come to see me about a matter with which I could help him. I had been asked to come to city hall before, but this was the first time anyone had asked me for help with city business.

A few days later, I greeted Roger and Jason Brady, public information officer for the city of Fayetteville. They explained that the city was applying for an All-America City Award. Fayetteville last enjoyed that designation in 1985, when an aggressive program of purchasing downtown properties transformed the inner city from an infamous skid row environment of bars and strip joints to a more wholesome atmosphere of public services and small businesses. As I listened to them describe the thorough application process for this coveted designation, I was surprised to learn of its prestige. I had seen the red, white, and blue "All-America City" signs as I traveled around the country, but I thought they were rather common political prizes, given by governors to reward communities for supporting them in elections. Not so. Only ten cities or towns in the entire country receive the All-American City Award each year. This was no small thing.

These men said they had identified three unique develop-ments in Fayetteville they believed to be noteworthy. These developments could form the cornerstones of the city's application for an All-American City Award. They included "Study Circles," a program of racial reconciliation (one group of which took place in our church); "Metro-Visions," a model program of collaboration involving various segments of the city; and "Operation Inasmuch," the highly successful program of local, hands-on mission work our church had begun in Fayetteville. They came to ask me to provide a description of Operation Inasmuch to be included in Fayetteville's application for this prestigious award.

Some of the criteria for this award are the following:

- Participation of the public, private, and nonprofit sectors and key constituencies to the maximum extent possible
- Projects that address the community's most important needs
- Clear demonstration of project results and impacts—for example, dollars raised or number of people affected[3]

When was the last time you remember a city official asking a pastor or church official to tell him what the church is doing that is making such a difference in the community? In twenty-seven years of ministry, it had *never* happened to me, nor can I remember any of my colleagues in ministry sharing such a thing.

Several months later at a raucous celebration in downtown Atlanta, Fayetteville was recognized as an All-America City. Operation Inasmuch drew the attention of the panel of judges from the United Civil League, which sponsored this competition each year. During the questioning from the panel, it was noted that this program is an example of the faith-based initiatives President George W. Bush had been encouraging since he took office in 2001.

This story shows that Operation Inasmuch has come of age. No longer is it the activity of a single congregation that gets lost in the hustle and bustle of a diverse, urban community. It has become a community-wide happening. No longer is it thought of as an occasional blitz of a few do-gooders making what splash they can in a world that hardly notices selfless service. It has become a major point of pride in a community that has suffered from a poor self-image for a long time. Finally, the church is doing what we should have been doing all along—getting outside the walls of our buildings to carry the love and grace of God to people who need it the most. And the rest of the community has noticed the difference we are making.

This was the second time Operation Inasmuch has been acknowledged by government officials as worthy of recognition. In 1998 the North Carolina Governor's Summit on America's

Promise and Volunteerism named Operation Inasmuch as one of eight "Exemplary Programs," the only church-related program in the state of North Carolina to be given this distinction. To be selected as one of eight—out of 142 volunteer programs throughout the state—helped put Operation Inasmuch on the map.

The criteria for an Exemplary Program in this summit reveals the level of effectiveness Operation Inasmuch had achieved in just three years. The *Summit Journal* lists the criteria as follows:

- Effectively mobilize volunteers or utilize community service as a solution to meeting a community's greatest needs
- Demonstrate methods of effective collaboration
- Demonstrate effective use of diverse resources
- Show measurable success on a state, local, or neighborhood level

A letter from Governor Hunt's Office on Citizen Affairs accompanied the certificate of recognition. The letter included these comments:

We launched this initiative to bring to the fore work programs and practices that are making a difference in North Carolina…The stories you shared are both moving and educational. The presenters on the exemplary panels, who spoke during the workshop session, left memories that continue to ripple through conversation throughout the state.[4]

Clearly, recognition is not the reason for doing Operation Inasmuch, and any church that launches this ministry for that purpose is likely to be disappointed. On the other hand, churches suffer from underexposure more than overexposure. In a world where crime and corruption get more than their fair share of headlines, it is good to know the church has not lost all of its influence just yet. Most pastors and congregational leaders will find it encouraging to know that people in powerful positions still appreciate decent folk helping neighbors they do not know just because they have a need.

The Start of Something Big

The original language of the New Testament has two words for time—*chronos* and *kairos*. The first refers to the ticking of the clock. It is the word from which we derive our words *chronology, chronicles,* and so forth. The second word refers to unrepeatable moments when something happens that becomes a benchmark for a person's or a group's life. Often these special moments are not recognized as such for a while. Only after some time has passed, providing the benefit of hindsight, is one able to reflect on the significance of that moment. That's the way I remember now my first date with the girl who would become my wife. It was a very enjoyable time, but not a "love at first sight" experience. However, love sprouted like a spring flower over the weeks that followed, and we married two-and-a-half years later. Only then did I come to see our first romantic encounter as a *kairos* moment in my life.

That is what happened with the first Operation Inasmuch. At the time neither I nor anyone else involved in its inception saw it as something that would transform our congregation, much less have such an impact on our community and other communities as I have already described in this chapter. God did not send the plans for it on tablets of stone. We enjoyed no mystical prayer meeting in which God's Spirit moved as at Pentecost. Such an event would make for an exciting story, but it would not be true.

On the other hand, how Operation Inasmuch began furnishes us a lesson: You never know what God has in mind when you are faithful in what seems to be the routine tasks of ministry. That which appears to us to be rather ordinary may, in fact, have the potential of the extraordinary. A ministry designed to be a one-time event with a limited scope may be something God intends to use to revitalize his church. As you read the story of how Operation Inasmuch came about, take heart.

Routine tasks of ministry have a way of draining us. At their worst, such tasks lead us to question whether God might be willing to let us do something else. But in the *kairos* moment these tasks may, in fact, be the beginning of something big.

Operation Inasmuch began at a staff retreat. Our ministerial staff retreated to the beach each September to discuss issues that we never had enough time to deal with in our everyday routines. During the retreat we planned the church calendar. In my first retreat with the staff at Snyder Memorial in 1994, we talked about our desire to see the congregation renewed. The church had a lot of energy at the time. A new pastor had come; and the honeymoon was in full swing, but we knew it would not last indefinitely. We discussed innovative ways of renewing the church, admitting to one another that the traditional "revival" or series of evangelistic meetings would not likely get the job done.

Someone suggested it might be effective to get the church away from the campus in some sort of ministry. Another shared a story about a Baptist church in North Carolina canceling their Sunday morning service to do mission work in their community. The creative juices were beginning to flow. Before we knew it, we had decided to challenge our congregation to do a one-day mission blitz in Fayetteville in March of 1995. I suggested that since Fayetteville is a military town, we should call it Operation Inasmuch, based on the Matthew 25 passage in which Jesus said, "Inasmuch as you did it to one of the least of these my brethren, you did it to me" (NKJV). We agreed that the missions committee of the church should be tasked with planning the day of hands-on projects and that the staff would plan special services leading up to that day. The services would be designed to mobilize and motivate our members to get involved. And with that we were off and running.

I had some experience with local volunteer mission work in other churches, but I had never taken this approach. I was intrigued by the concept of doing multiple mission projects in one day. I hoped we would involve a significant portion of our active members, but I could not have anticipated the huge success it turned out to be.

A Convergence of Ministry and Vision

Simultaneous to the planning for the first Operation Inasmuch, our congregation was undertaking a visioning process. In support of that effort, I preached a series of sermons concerning the role of vision with God's people: "Write the Vision, Make It Plain" (Hab. 2); "God's Vision Is Adventurous" (Gen. 12); "God's Vision Is Perilous" (Ex. 3); "God's Vision Is Persistent" (Josh. 14); "God's Vision Is Emboldening" (Acts 4); and "God's Vision Colors outside the Lines" (Acts 9). As you can see from the titles of those sermons, I was challenging the congregation to stretch their thinking about church, to get beyond the traditions to see what God might want to do with Snyder in the last years of the twentieth century. Unwittingly, these messages had the effect of preparing the congregation for Operation Inasmuch. They had not yet learned about it, but the soil of their souls was being prepared like winter plowing weeks before the planting season. I did not see the relationship between the visioning process and Operation Inasmuch at the time, but I and everyone else would soon make that discovery.

The day came for the visioning committee to write a vision statement. We set aside an entire day for the task and went off campus to do it. We began that day with an extensive time of prayer and sharing. Then we set about our task. No group ever worked more diligently on a task than we did, but at the end of the day we had to admit to each other that we did not have a finished product. One simple sentence was all we wanted, and we could not find it. We were disappointed, to say the least, but to our credit we refused to accept an inferior product just to say we had finished our assignment.

One week later, Operation Inasmuch took place. Hundreds of Snyder members of all ages, about 75 percent of our average attendance, spread out over Fayetteville repairing homes, building wheelchair ramps, holding backyard Bible clubs in government housing areas, sewing lap robes for nursing home patients, assembling Easter baskets to be given to low-income children, and replacing roofs. It was the most exhilarating event I have witnessed in a church. The church was renewed for sure. Fellowship was strengthened. Commitment to mission work was expanded exponentially.

Furthermore, we discovered that God had given us a gift. He had given us a way to get outside the walls of our buildings to touch some of our neighbors at their point of need. He had empowered many who had never been involved in mission work to see their skills of carpentry or sewing or playing with children as tools in the hands of God himself. In addition to these, we discovered that God had also given our congregation a new vision. When we arrived at church the next day, Sunday, the enthusiasm of the previous day had not subsided at all. If anything, enthusiasm surged even more as we gathered together again. To a person, each member of the visioning committee I saw that day said: "*That* (referring to Operation Inasmuch) is what God wants us to do!" The next week we adopted a vision statement almost without discussion. That statement embodied our experience from the previous week. It gives priority to local, hands-on mission work. It stated that "every member of Snyder Memorial…is to be a missionary."

Ministry and vision had converged. Sometimes God gives his people a vision so they see where God is taking them. This happened with the Israelites trekking across the desert toward the promised land. In such times God's people are driven by their vision of what God has promised them. Other times God leads his people into experiences that produce for them a new vision, such as happened with the infant church in Jerusalem. As they huddled together in prayer in Jerusalem, God sent his Spirit to empower and mobilize them as the church of Jesus Christ. Those disillusioned followers of Jesus went to that familiar place confused and scared without any sense of direction despite Jesus' challenge that they serve as his witnesses. They left empowered and mobilized. Their experience of the outpouring of God's Spirit gave them a vision that continues to this day.

This was our experience with Operation Inasmuch— experience led to vision. What began as a creative approach to church renewal became a revolution that has no end in sight. Congregations go for decades without experiencing the empowerment of God. So, when such empowerment does happen, the church is not likely to forget. For our congregation Operation Inasmuch is more than a one-day mission blitz into our community. It is like the stone tablets containing the covenant with God for the people of ancient Israel: It defines who we are. God has strategically brought us to the understanding that we are not here primarily for ourselves but to impact our community for him. He used ministry in the present to show us the shape of the future.

Our church has no doubt that all this has been of God. This conviction is not based so much on our experiences, although they surely have been persuasive for us, as on what we have seen take place in other churches and communities. It is my belief that when something is of God, it has application to many different people in various situations. This is precisely what has happened with Operation Inasmuch. As many as three dozen churches in Fayetteville now participate in Operation Inasmuch twice a year. Approximately four hundred churches have conducted an Operation Inasmuch in four states. As it spreads from church to church, we have no way of recording all the churches involved. The next chapter will share some of the stories of the impact Operation Inasmuch has had on individual believers, congregations, and communities.

Here is one for now. As I was writing these words, I received a phone call from a pastor in a Baptist church in a small community just north of Winston-Salem, North Carolina. He verified that his church has conducted several Operation Inasmuch events, which date back prior to his term as pastor. When I told him I was writing a book about Operation

Inasmuch, he shared that he appeared before that congregation on a Wednesday evening in view of a call to be their pastor. That Saturday was their Operation Inasmuch. When he saw the number of people who had signed up—170 out of a total membership of about 250—he was, in his own words, "sold on the church." Every time I hear a story like this, the conviction that Operation Inasmuch is of God is reaffirmed again.

The mission of the church has not changed since the first century. What has changed countless times is the method of accomplishing that mission. Operation Inasmuch offers no new task for the church, but it does offer an effective way of doing an old task, namely being the hands and feet of God in a broken world. Matthew 25:40 is still in effect: "Inasmuch as you did [ministry] to one of the least of these my brethren, you did it to me" (NKJV). Or, as Esther Burroughs puts it:

> We are to be God's hands in day care, his justice in the job bank, his mercy in the car pool, his comfort in the shelter, his provision in the food lines, and his compassion in the streets. When we feed others, we are feeding him. When we clothe others, we clothe him. When we find them a job or home, we are doing that in his name.[5]

2

Transforming Believers and Congregations

The best way to find yourself is to lose yourself in the service of others.

MAHATMA GANDHI

We make a living by what we get. We make a life by what we give.

WINSTON CHURCHILL

One measure of an event or program's success is its application. If it applies to many different people in various circumstances and places, then it is deemed successful. This is true for nonreligious groups as well as churches. However, the church has additional criteria for success: Does the event or program advance the kingdom of God? Does it edify the church? Does it have transformational power? By all these criteria Operation Inasmuch has been successful. It has worked in many different

15

settings, and all reports indicate that it has passed the more stringent tests of effective ministry.

Operation Inasmuch has been a useful tool in empowering congregations and individual believers to touch others with the love of God. As already acknowledged, Operation Inasmuch is not so much a novel ministry as it is an effective way of involving more people and accomplishing more in missions. In every case in which a church has conducted an Operation Inasmuch, that church was already offering helpful ministry to its community. Operation Inasmuch has broadened the church's effectiveness in several ways.

In this chapter I share some of the stories of churches' and individuals' experiences with Operation Inasmuch. Through interviews, letters, and e-mails, I have gathered a mountain of data on this subject. As much as anything this book can share, these stories and comments verify the validity of Operation Inasmuch.

I received the following letter from Mike Moser, layperson at Mars Hill Baptist Church in western North Carolina, about a month after his church conducted their first Operation Inasmuch. Mars Hill is a small-town, college church with an average attendance of 250.

> Mars Hill Baptist Church has completed our first Operation Inasmuch. On behalf of all involved in our project, we thank you…for bringing this project to us.
>
> The project was a great success. We had over 260 people involved in 17 different projects, with ages ranging from two-year-olds stuffing care packages, to high school and college kids doing a little bit of everything, to an eighty-eight-year-old assisting in operations at the church. We are very pleased at the number of people we were able to involve who have not been active in outreach ministry or church.
>
> Our range of projects included everything from a Bible study for kids conducted by our youth at the local

housing project, sewing over 75 walker bags, gowns, and bed pads for local nursing homes and hospice, to several different construction projects. Our construction projects included three handicap ramps at homes for elderly to major renovations, new kitchen countertops, plumbing repairs, and clean up at the county Helpmate home for abused women.

Even an especially cold morning provided an opportunity to serve and fellowship in delivering coffee and hot chocolate to those working outside. Some great witnessing and sharing of faith took place as God led our people through this opportunity. The timing of our event resulted in many from our community assisting victims in the Hurricane Floyd [relief] effort as well as "Make a Difference Day" that weekend. Instead of diminishing our efforts, these efforts further mobilized, not only our church, but also other churches, civic organizations, and Mars Hill College students. Truly more people in Madison County...were involved in helping others and serving the Lord than in a long time.

We have already held an evaluation meeting and plan to conduct this project again. We are also working on developing a resource bank of gifts and talents to be able to better respond to short-term individual and community needs in addition to OIAM as a yearly project. Our goals include encouraging other churches to adopt Operation Inasmuch. We welcome any opportunity to share this project and look forward to talking with you soon as to how we can expand this means of fulfilling the "Great Commission."

This letter says it well. Operation Inasmuch has made a lasting impression on the Mars Hill Baptist Church and Mars Hill community. Since this letter, the church has conducted two more Operation Inasmuch events, with increased participation. They have begun to include other congregations as well.

It Works

Operation Inasmuch has appealed to so many churches for several reasons. In conversations with dozens of congregational leaders, the same themes surfaced again and again as to why it works and why word about Operation Inasmuch is spreading.

One, it is a focused, one-day event. Most church folk are stretched pretty thin these days. Not only are they staffing all the numerous volunteer positions in their churches, but they are often also active in civic organizations, volunteering at the local hospital, helping out at the community clothes closet, and so on. Consequently, they are reluctant to commit to a long-term project. However, they will consider getting involved in a project that can be completed in one day. People will give a whole Saturday a couple of times a year, but they will avoid the weekly or even monthly commitment that does not already have a strong attraction for them. As one church coordinator put it: "It's almost like a missions bullet…In our society and I would say in our church, it's hard for people to fit into their busy schedule a long-term commitment for a lot of different things. [Operation Inasmuch] allows us to do mission work, and it's nothing you have to sign up for months or years or whatever."[1]

Two, it is local. Americans have a strong bias toward anything local. The Gallup Organization encounters this bias regularly as they survey opinions of Americans on a broad range of issues.[2] In part because the national media influences us negatively toward the state of things far away, and in part because we naturally have more confidence in and affinity toward those things, people, or organizations we know personally, we prefer to give ourselves to local causes.

The practical side of involving people in mission work is it must be accessible to them. A few people are so moved to get involved in missions that they will go almost anywhere to do it, but most will not. However, when the opportunity is on the other side of their town or around the corner, more people will consider it. Local missions has a special appeal to younger Christians. As I will discuss in greater detail in chapter 4, "Baby

Boomers" and "Busters" are not as likely to be supportive of mission causes in faraway places. They prefer doing mission work in their own community. Operation Inasmuch appeals to the local-minded. One participant had this to say:

> We should do the faraway things, but you don't feel and know firsthand those faraway things. You're not responsible. But if you're living in a community and realize you're blessed, you should return something to the community. It makes me feel good to do this. I work from forty to fifty hours a week. I have two children and a husband. I have lots of things I do, but I do these mission things, too, because it makes me feel really, really good.[3]

Three, it is hands-on. For all our participation in checkbook missions, many prefer to get personally involved. They want to see and hear and touch the work themselves. They enjoy seeing the results of their labors. I believe the underlying motive here is the desire to make a difference, to know that something we have done makes this a better world or community in which to live. The personal involvement of Operation Inasmuch does more to help Christians see they are making a difference than anything else. Consider the comments of one volunteer who took meals to elderly persons in her community:

> Many of the people we visited had been unable to come to church or any community functions for quite some time. They were thrilled to learn the latest happenings in our community. Their eyes would sparkle at the mention of a friend they hadn't seen in some time or some past memory. By the time we left, their cheeks were rosy, and their smiles were genuine. When the eight of us met back at the church for lunch, we all felt blessed and humbled. How little it takes to make a person happy…not a lot of time, effort, or money![4]

Four, the methodology is already in place. Congregational leaders are like the circus sideshow in which the entertainer spins plates on long sticks. The more plates he starts spinning, the harder he has to work to keep them going. So it is with congregational leaders reading of yet another program for them to keep spinning. They want to know whether the methods are tried and true and whether they can implement the program with a minimum of experimentation on their part. Here is the good news: the "nuts and bolts" of Operation Inasmuch have already been worked out. Chapter 8 will walk the reader through the entire process of planning and implementing an Operation Inasmuch. While there is freedom for any church to modify the plan to fit their particular situation, the basics are proven. One coordinator agreed: "We were able to be part of an operation whereby the doors were open that we could help the community easily. When you want to help the community and you don't have a vehicle, then you have to start from scratch to get them to have confidence in you."[5] Another said: "The beauty of it was that it was already in place and we didn't have to reinvent the wheel."[6]

Five, the cost is affordable. Sooner or later, every church event is evaluated in terms of its cost. Most churches have been able to undertake Operation Inasmuch without having budgetary support in place. Costs are often shared with other nonprofit organizations or churches or, in some cases, government entities. When a church has to bear most of the costs of their Operation Inasmuch, they usually find this is not a burdensome expense. Costs average beten $6 and $10 per volunteer depending on partnerships with community agencies, who often provide materials for projects.

Six, it offers something for everyone. Mike Moser's letter makes this point. The plan for Operation Inasmuch calls for projects to be offered for every age group in a congregation. This is the key to widespread participation. Every church has people who honestly believe they lack gifts that can be useful in ministry. These people neither teach classes nor sing in the choir nor serve on committees; but many of them have carpentry skills, or a talent for sewing, or something that can be used in Operation

Inasmuch. In response to the question of why Operation Inasmuch was so successful in her church, a leader said: "Mainly because it has gotten people involved. They are able to use their gifts in areas they have not been able to use them before."[7] A volunteer adds: "Some people have the idea that they do not have anything that can be used in ministry. I'm a prime example. We would have classes on spiritual gifts, and I didn't think I had any gift worthwhile. Now I've discovered through [Operation Inasmuch] that I have gifts to be used in the church."[8]

Seven, it facilitates brotherhood. As one leader confessed: "The thing that is most appealing to me is the community focus and the ecumenical effort. [We] Baptists are traditionally isolationists in the way we do life. Some of that is arrogance; some of it is theology. I like our people having the opportunity to join with others."[9] It is this feature of Operation Inasmuch more than any other—bringing people of different races and faith systems together—that has gotten the attention of community leaders and led to the recognitions described in chapter 1.

As a pastor, I am naturally suspicious of new ideas that are reputed to be *the* turnaround program for the church, so I make no such claim for Operation Inasmuch. However, I am persuaded by the overwhelming evidence from personal conversations and letters that this is a tool that has the potential to help many congregations get better at some things they are already doing. In the remainder of this chapter I will share additional testimony as to its value to congregations and individual believers.

Impact on Congregations

Do you remember the criteria for a successful event in churches mentioned at the beginning of this chapter? Two of those questions—Does it edify the church? and, Does it have transformational power?—are always on a congregational leader's mind when considering whether to take the risks that are inherent in anything new in church life. That Operation Inasmuch is spreading from church to church indicates that it does, in fact, build up and transform congregations. Experience shows that it impacts churches in seven ways.

One, it mobilizes large numbers of people. Participation in churches ranges from 25 percent on the low end, to 125 percent of average weekly attendance on the high end, depending on the number of projects offered and the quality of planning and recruitment. The median level of involvement usually falls between 50 and 75 percent of average attendance. Most churches that have that level of participation in any event would consider it a huge success.

Congregations that have partnered with other congregations in an Operation Inasmuch have experienced another benefit in that they are encouraged to see so many fellow believers, often of other denominations, working together to meet people's basic needs. One coordinator put it well: "It's wonderful to see many people working together. It's heartening. The volunteers say, 'We're not alone. There is a great army of God at work out here!'"[10]

Two, it energizes a congregation. Operation Inasmuch has been a catalyst for church renewal. This is due in part to the sheer numbers of people involved. Such involvement tends to generate its own excitement. Renewal is also due to the nature of doing for others. This was our experience in the first Operation Inasmuch at Snyder Memorial, and it has been repeated dozens of times as other congregations have conducted their own event. Here is one of many witnesses: "Our day devoted to helping people at their point of need resulted in spiritual growth for most everyone who participated…Members experienced a spiritual renewal and continued commitment to respond to the needs of others in our community. Our eyes have become open and our heart more sensitive to others' needs."[11] Another says: "Any time you are reminded of the bigness of God and the largeness of the community of faith beyond your own people in your own building, you are affirmed in your commitment to God. To me it is an expression of worship that is…praising God through the sound of hammers and sawing and literally building homes, but in a greater sense building the kingdom of God."[12]

Another benefit of Operation Inasmuch also relates to its ability to energize a congregation. This benefit is its potential to strengthen families. Some churches encourage families to work together on a project, providing valuable bonding and teaching opportunities. A father of two grade-school-age daughters reports that his family always works together. This experience has led quite naturally to teachable moments that might not come any other way. One church coordinator tells how Operation Inasmuch has become a way to honor a member of their family:

> We have a young man whose wife died. She had cancer, and the church was praying for her recovery. A short time after she learned she had cancer, she came and worked on the new Directions project with her husband and two daughters. A lot of people saw that and said, "If she can get involved, so can I." She died before the next Operation Inasmuch, but every year her husband and daughters show up. They don't get involved in a lot of other things in the church, but they do with Operation Inasmuch. They honor their wife/mother by doing that.[13]

Three, it builds fellowship. Operation Inasmuch often teams people together who would not ordinarily spend time with one another. As a result of working together for a day, they build a friendship that carries over into the larger church life. One coordinator sees it as an effective way for new members to become assimilated into the fellowship: "[New members] were our most willing workers and came with much enthusiasm to be involved in their church family. Working with people they did not know opened doors for new friendships and gave them a feeling of belonging."[14]

Another describes his church's experience of building a playground at a local school attended by at-risk students. A steady rain fell that day. "We were all soaking wet and filthy dirty and having a great time. People who really never saw each other were laughing and cutting up with each other, throwing mud and stuff at each other. It really was a fellowship-building thing."[15]

Although it may not be a deliberate strategy to use Operation Inasmuch as a healing agent for a fragmented fellowship, occasionally it turns out that way. One congregation that was reeling from the sudden and unpleasant departure of two ministers found new common ground in their experience with hands-on ministry. One of their volunteers puts it this way:

> There was a gulf a mile wide. We were busy dwelling on hurts real or imagined, pointing fingers, and concentrating on negative thoughts. [Operation Inasmuch] gave us something positive to dwell on. [It] had a great healing effect. You can't stay mad when you're working side by side hammering, sawing, painting, raking, etc., doing God's work.[16]

Another church had its fellowship mended through an Operation Inasmuch:

> I firmly believe God sent the first Operation Inasmuch into our midst at a time when we needed a unifying experience in our fellowship, because fellowship was waning. It did the trick! If I had to choose any one ministry that would revitalize a congregation, bring old friends back together, and alert us to the many needs around us, it would have to be Operation Inasmuch.[17]

Some congregations have added members because of Operation Inasmuch. One reported that a young woman first volunteered for their Operation Inasmuch and was so impressed with her experience that she joined the church. Other churches have reported similar experiences. One congregation has added two new believers through Operation Inasmuch. Their friends who were church members already invited them to help with a project. This prompted their interest in spiritual matters and eventually opened them to the gospel and led to church membership.[18]

Four, it broadens a congregation's understanding of missions. Too many believers think of missions strictly as something that takes place in a Third World setting. Operation Inasmuch brings that perception into a church's backyard. Here are a couple of testimonies: "We've always been a missions-minded church, but helping people realize that missions happens right across the street and down the road, in the school next door and those kinds of things as opposed to missionaries coming in [has been an educational experience].[19] "Operation Inasmuch helped open our congregation's eyes to the many needs around us…Missions can be fun and not as scary when you can use your natural abilities to do it. Often people are willing to help if they know of a specific need, and Operation Inasmuch is a good vehicle to help people plug in."[20]

Five, it enhances involvement in other mission causes. Our own congregation has seen a sharp increase in missions involvement since we began Operation Inasmuch, from a local ministry to the homeless, to an ongoing carpentry ministry, to more persons making overseas mission trips. This has been the experience of other congregations as well. One coordinator describes this impact of Operation Inasmuch as the development of a "missions can-do attitude" in her church.[21] A leader in an African American church says: "Some people have been reluctant to get involved because of the fear of the unknown. Through Operation Inasmuch, they have seen that these are people in need, not people who will hurt them, and that has changed the way they respond. Whenever we say we need clothing or food for the needy, we don't have to beg the way we used to; it just comes."[22] In response to a question regarding the benefits of Operation Inasmuch, one pastor said: "Our people got turned on to missions. Now we've taken a mission trip to Honduras, and everyone who went was involved in Operation Inasmuch."[23]

Involvement in hands-on mission work has a way of stimulating one's creativity. Clearly, the more people we can get involved the more creative approaches to ministry will be generated. Such was the experience of one woman of Ardmore

Baptist Church, Winston-Salem, North Carolina, who discovered another world of needs when she participated in a project at a nearby elementary school. Here is her story.

> I decided to reach out to Latham Elementary School and see if they would accept me as a reading tutor for a few children. Each day from 1:00 to 3:00 I had four third-grade children who formed a circle and read with me. When the children complained that what we were reading was boring, I wrote stories of my own, stories about what it was like in the old days when I was a kid. They could not wait for the next story. I put them together to form a book and gave each child a copy. We took a field trip to the places in the book—my childhood home, the stores where I shopped as a child, the school I attended (now a church). The children drew the pictures to illustrate the stories I wrote and they are included in my book.[24]

Here are examples of other congregational endeavors as a result of their involvement in Operation Inasmuch:

- hurricane relief (Lafayette Baptist Church, Fayetteville, North Carolina; First Baptist Church, Smithfield, North Carolina)
- starting a Kid's Café serving at-risk students a nourishing meal and helping them with their homework three nights a week (Ardmore Baptist Church, Winston-Salem, North Carolina)
- gathering more than a thousand blankets for Bosnia (Beverly Hills Baptist Church, Asheville, North Carolina)
- making and distributing "quillows" (quilts [or blankets] that fold into pillows) for disabled and disturbed children, through the local Department of Social Services (First Baptist Church, Marion, North Carolina)

When you read this list of new ministries begun by local congregations, is it any wonder that so many have said "Operation Inasmuch is a God thing"?

Six, it authenticates a Christian witness. The debate as to which should be given higher priority—evangelism or so-called social ministries—is a false choice. They go together. At its best, hands-on ministry to persons in need opens the way for evangelism. In each Operation Inasmuch Snyder Memorial conducts, we have a team of volunteers who visit personally with the recipients of all the projects, sharing the gospel of God's love in Christ with them. It is the easiest witnessing encounter anyone can have. You had better believe that when a person is having a new roof put on their home by volunteers from a church, the occupants of that house will listen to a gospel presentation.

One congregation is intentional about this aspect of their ministry with Operation Inasmuch. They leave a card with everyone they touch in their work. The card says:

> What we have done for you today, we have done because of our love for the Lord Jesus Christ. If you, too, believe in Him, all we ask is that you would follow our example and serve someone else in His name. If you do not know Jesus, we simply ask that you would consider attending church to find out about the One who has motivated us to minister freely in His name today.[25]

Because this aspect of Operation Inasmuch is so important, I want to share two stories I uncovered in the course of researching congregations' experiences with it. Both validate the claim that fresh opportunities to witness to the transformational power of the gospel come through hands-on ministry. The first is from Violet Smith of Germanton Baptist Church, Germanton, North Carolina:

> My husband, Charlie, and a group of our men were building a wheelchair ramp in a trailer park in what turned out to be a rather undesirable place. While there, Charlie was asked to come inside and talk to a young man who worked at the park and had come by to see what was going on. They were accustomed to seeing

police cars, not church vans. The young man was in trouble and needed someone to talk to. Charlie was able to witness to him and, by way of their listening, to others in the trailer. Through follow-up visits in his family's home, the young man eventually accepted Christ. As we say, we are planting seeds most of the time and do not know what the outcome may be. We always pray with people and leave them a brochure explaining who we are, why we are doing these things, and the plan of salvation; but we often don't know what the fruit may be.[26]

This second story is from Keith Breedlove of First Baptist Church, Morganton, North Carolina:

My personal story revolves around a boy named Dustin. A few of the men in our class helped put a tin roof over a mobile home for a lady. We got there on Friday night to get an early start. There was a ten-year-old boy, her grandson, who kept hanging around and wanting to help out. Mostly he wanted attention. I told our group that without a doubt, the boy would be there on Saturday when we came back. Before heading out on Saturday to the work site, I got a children's Bible from our Minister of Education. As expected, Dustin was there hanging around. He helped, talked, watched, and asked questions. I knew that our job was more than roof work.

At lunch time, our project leader's wife came with pizza. She ended up staying a long time talking with Dustin and his grandmother. She came up to me and said that Dustin was asking about the Lord and what it meant to become a Christian. So she and I talked with him to see where he was spiritually. I told her that we had a Bible for him. We gave him the Bible and told him how to go about reading it. We also gave his grandmother a Bible.

A few weeks later we went back for a visit to see if he was ready to accept the Lord. His grandmother did tell us that he had been reading his Bible, but he did not seem to be ready for a commitment. All along another member of our church had been talking to him at school. She is a teacher and was his mentor. Some time later, Dustin went to her room and told her that he wanted to accept Jesus as Savior. She prayed with him to accept the Lord.[27]

Seven, it gives laypersons prominence in ministry. It is no exaggeration to say that in many churches ministry has become the well-guarded turf of professional ministers. We (I am one!) want our parishioners to support the work of the church with their attendance and money, but we often expect them to leave the really important stuff to us. After all, we *are* the experts. But in Operation Inasmuch the roles are reversed—laypersons are the experts, and we are the amateurs. Says one coordinator: "The quiet, introverted electrician who doesn't fit in the church's committee structure will get in there and get involved. When he's on site, he knows what he's doing. He is affirmed for what he's doing. People are looking to him for leadership."[28]

Sometimes new congregational leaders emerge through the unique opportunity of Operation Inasmuch. One church reports that a sixty-year-old carpenter who had no experience in leadership positions has now been selected to serve as a deacon largely because of his involvement in Operation Inasmuch. One of his ministers says: "Gene is an example of one person who has gotten turned on to missions through [Operation Inasmuch]. His attitude now is if anyone needs what he can do for them, he's glad to do it any time."[29]

I usually work on a roofing project. My members get a kick out of watching me do that kind of work. I can hold my own in driving nails, but I need help with some of the more specialized parts of the job. I show up in an old pair of overalls because I know that will get a laugh from them, but they respect the fact that I am willing to "get down and dirty" with them. I am convinced that how the roles play out in a roofing project of Operation Inasmuch is closer to the way Jesus intended for the kingdom of God to be in the first place.

Impact on Individuals

Operation Inasmuch is a group effort, and in some cases where several churches in a community form a partnership, it is a multigroup effort. But every group is composed of individuals who band together to accomplish a common goal. Although there was some sign of Operation Inasmuch's impact on individuals in the previous section, I want to zoom in on that aspect in this section.

In talking or corresponding with persons from many different congregations that have done an Operation Inasmuch, several benefits to individual participants surface again and again. The most commonly heard benefit is the fortifying of one's faith. A sixteen-year-old says: "To try to explain how Operation Inasmuch affected my life is completely impossible. I have been on several youth mission trips and done other work in the community with various mission teams, however, my Inasmuch experiences left an impression on my life unlike any other."[30] Sue Byrd of Snyder Memorial expresses the feeling of many who participate in Operation Inasmuch: "I've gained a new appreciation for Jesus' words 'It is more blessed to give than to receive.' Not only because we're doing what we've been commanded to do, but in every instance of giving, I've been the one who left feeling, 'God really used these people to minister to me!'"[31] The same sentiment is echoed by the patron saint of hands-on ministry, Mother Teresa: "Only in heaven will we see how much we owe to the poor for helping us love God better because of them."[32]

A dramatic example of the spiritual impact of Operation Inasmuch is the turnaround of a young man named Joel. Joel grew up in a churchgoing family, but when he became an adult, he dropped out. He maintained a loose connection with the church but did not feel comfortable in that setting. The one thing he was comfortable with was using his hands. When he heard about a one-day, hands-on, mission blitz to be done by his church, he signed up. Working with church folk was more enjoyable than he expected. In a few weeks he ventured out to attend worship. Some of the members with whom he had worked in Operation Inasmuch gave him a friendly slap on the back. He came back. Today Joel sings in the choir, serves on the missions committee, and has gone to Honduras to build homes for people displaced by the devastating floods of 1999.

Joel's experience shows the connection between a person's hands and his heart. When Joel used his hands in God's work, God touched his heart.

Another story of transformation is that of Donald, an angry, African American young man. An Operation Inasmuch was conducted in his neighborhood. However, the home where he lived did not qualify to be one of the projects. Even so, a group from one of the churches that worked in that neighborhood recognized the need and asked to take it on at another time. Donald was out of work and flirting with crime at the time, but the men of that church adopted him and got him involved in helping with the repairs to his home. Slowly, his attitude softened. He ceased to look beyond his front door for excitement and began to anticipate his new friends coming to work on his home.

During that period of time, the men from the church came one day and found Donald in bed sick. When they investigated, they saw that he needed immediate medical attention and called an ambulance. He was admitted into the local hospital. The doctor who attended to him told the volunteers later that he might not have survived if he had not gotten to the hospital when he did. Now he is healthy and living in a home of which he is proud. Furthermore, a local plumber has hired him (one who is also involved in Operation Inasmuch), and he is regularly involved in worship and other church activities of the congregation that reached out to him. Donald was transformed by the love of God, extended by people who met him through an Operation Inasmuch.[33]

Operation Inasmuch impacts individual believers in another way. Often when they move outside the walls of their church buildings, their eyes are opened to the harsh realities of poverty and loneliness. Their perception of people in need undergoes an overhaul. A leader in a middle-class, African American congregation says: "Our members did not know that people live in Fayetteville without indoor plumbing or looking at the ground through their floor. We put blinders on."[34] Operation Inasmuch has removed the blinders of hundreds of believers because they have become personally involved in the lives of people living in circumstances very different from their own.

Operation Inasmuch is a train that travels on the skills of ordinary believers. Its appeal is that it offers opportunities for Christians to use their talents for the Kingdom. Ministry is too narrowly defined as those skills that are most visible in church life—teaching, preaching, singing, or presiding over meetings. We seem to forget that the New Testament gives a different picture, one of God using persons with so-called secular skills to do his work: fishermen, doctors, tentmakers, businesswomen, and so forth. When laypersons discover that their skills can be used to render ministry in Jesus' name, their whole concept of ministry changes. They finally begin to receive the fulfillment of being used by God to help others. A schoolteacher in our congregation looks forward to the sewing project each Operation Inasmuch. She says: "Come the springtime, I am sure that I will be signing up again for sewing. There are many things I physically cannot do due to severe problems with my back, but I know that I can spend a day sewing for others."[35] I submit that a needle and thread are just as apt tools for ministry as a Bible and commentaries are.

Kim Kincer is on the faculty of Methodist College in Fayetteville and an active member of Snyder Memorial. She participates in Operation Inasmuch every time it is conducted there. In one event she worked at a block party where she entertained young children who came to see what was happening. There was a young African American girl "hanging around." She would come close to Kim, then retreat quickly when Kim attempted to engage her in conversation. Finally she got the girl to tell her name—Chyadija. When the block party was winding down, Kincer told the girl she'd like to visit her sometime. Chyadija said, "No you won't. You'll never see me again." Kincer made a decision right then to crack the hard shell the little girl had constructed to protect herself. She says, "I don't really know why, but something in me said this was a girl I could help."

That block party was in the fall of 2002. Kim Kincer and Chyadija have become fast friends. They go to the movies and to dinner. Kincer helps Chyadija with her homework. Kincer says, "In the early days, I couldn't get her to give me a hug, no matter what. Now there are times when she won't let go." She understands that this bond was made possible through Operation Inasmuch: "Mention Inasmuch, and people think about the hammers, the roofs, all that. But when you get to the heart of it, it's people and lives. It's a chance to reach out."

A story from Chuck Colson's prison ministry puts a neat bow on this chapter about the impact of hands-on ministry. "Prison Fellowship" supporters and volunteers accompanied him to an in-prison seminar. The event began in full view of the media, governor's proclamation and all. In the prison chapel, a popular gospel vocalist thrilled the "captive audience." Then a converted ex-convict gave his testimony. Finally, Colson spoke, challenging the prisoners to open themselves to the grace of God through Jesus Christ. The response was moving for even the most skeptical.

At the close of the seminar, one inmate stood and put the entire event in perspective. He said: "I really appreciated Chuck Colson's message, and I was stirred by Wintley Phipps's singing. Herman's testimony reached me where I was at. But, frankly, those things didn't impress me so much as the ladies among the volunteers who, after the crowd and the TV cameras left, went into the dining hall, with all the noise and confusion, and sat at the table to have a meal with us. That's what really got to me."[36] Operation Inasmuch enhances the possibility that ordinary believers can be used by God to do extraordinary things.

3

Hands-on Mission Helps Community

A civilization flourishes when people plant trees under which they will never sit.

GREEK PROVERB

I am of the opinion that my life belongs to the whole community and as long as I live it is my privilege to do for it whatever I can. I want to be thoroughly used up when I die.

GEORGE BERNARD SHAW

The headline read "Hands-on Mission Helps Community." The article described how Operation Inasmuch made an impact on Fayetteville, North Carolina. That impact came in two ways: in the projects that rendered help to persons at the point of their need, and in the collaboration of a white congregation and a black congregation in doing the work. The article featured eighty-nine-year-old Mary Moore, a widow confined to a wheelchair. She had no resources to repair the deterioration that had taken place in her home since her husband had died seven years earlier. Then volunteers from Operation Inasmuch showed up on a Saturday morning.

"They ripped off old shingles and replaced them," went the article. "Rotting fascia boards were replaced. Workers painted the outside of the house and made other repairs.

'I sure do appreciate them doing this for me,' said Ms. Moore. 'I think it's wonderful what they're doing.'"[1]

In this book I am making the point that God calls the church to get outside its walls to minister to people and that Operation Inasmuch is a viable model for doing that. The church has not done enough when congregations and individual believers are strengthened. The true test of mission endeavors is the difference they make in the world. Although it could not be demonstrated consistently by most churches' attitudes toward their communities, nevertheless it is true that a church exists for the benefit of the community, not for itself. Even a casual reading of the New Testament gives ample evidence of this truth. Yet it is surprising how little influence many churches have on their communities. For those congregational leaders searching for effective ways to expand their church's influence in their community, Operation Inasmuch may be the answer.

Impacting the Community in Four Ways

Operation Inasmuch churches have found four distinct ways they impact the community. *One, Operation Inasmuch helps other community agencies.* Every community has agencies, both faith-based and government-supported, whose purpose is to address the brokenness and basic needs of their citizens. Often these agencies function in isolation, without meaningful connections with other agencies or groups that share their purpose. Operation Inasmuch is designed to network with these already-established agencies, partnering with them to accomplish common goals. The result is a win-win proposition: The nonprofit agency is assisted in carrying out its mission as well as in broadening its constituency through the volunteers who assist it, and the congregation is provided an avenue of mission work through an established community ministry.

This relationship may take several directions—from simply expressing appreciation for those in the community who provide vital services, such as fire and safety personnel or medical personnel, to augmenting the work of agencies by providing volunteers to assist them. One church took baskets of fruit and cookies to all the firefighters; police officers; rescue squad personnel; Hospice, Ucare, and Crisis Center workers; and each shift of nurses in their community hospital. Another church prepared and distributed to all the nursing home personnel in its community thirty-day devotional guides offering encouragement for their generally thankless and often unpleasant jobs. You can be sure such simple, sincere expressions of love enhance the value of these churches in the eyes of their community.

Helping organizations never seem to have enough resources to do their work. They depend on volunteers, and any church that provides them is extending its influence deeper into its community. Operation Inasmuch has led to strong ties that bind between Fayetteville churches and the primary interdenominational benevolent agency—Fayetteville Urban Ministry. Rusty Long, Urban Ministry's executive director, describes the role of Operation Inasmuch in strengthening his organization's effectiveness: "Fayetteville Urban Ministry was started by a group of churches, and Operation Inasmuch has done more than anything to strengthen our ties with these churches. We are more ministry-focused now than before because of the increased involvement through Operation Inasmuch. It's putting us into the churches because Operation Inasmuch has increased our visibility and the churches want to know more about us."[2]

Rusty has discovered that Operation Inasmuch occasionally creates nice surprises. He says:

> After the Operation Inasmuch in October of 1999, a man walked into my office and laid the newspaper article

about that event on my desk. He asked: "Is this you?" I said: "Yes, that's something we're involved in." He said: "I have a check for you." And he handed me a check for $10,000. He said all the money had to go to fund these kinds of projects. He explained that this was a one-time gift since he'd just sold his business and wouldn't be able to do it again. That money paid for all the home repair projects of the next Operation Inasmuch. We wrote him a card about the next one and suggested that he might want to drive by. We never heard from him. However, he walked back in a year later and gave me another check for $5,000.[3]

Another local agency that has benefited from Operation Inasmuch is the Cumberland County Council on Older Adults. One of the primary functions of this organization is to provide wheelchair ramps for disabled persons who cannot provide such for themselves. Through Operation Inasmuch in Fayetteville, twenty-five wheelchair ramps have been constructed with volunteer help. Says Marty Buie, the council's director:

> Operation Inasmuch has really helped the Council on Older Adults…The volunteers make it possible for us to fulfill our mission easily…The recipients are ecstatic when they finally get access to and from their home by way of a brand new ramp. One woman who had been confined to her home for a very long time "went running up and down the ramp on her one good leg" when it was finished.[4]

I mentioned in the previous chapter the experience of Ardmore Baptist Church of Winston-Salem, North Carolina. They used Operation Inasmuch as an opportunity to establish an ongoing relationship with a nearby school heavily populated with students from low-income families. Once the congregation demonstrated their sincerity with the construction of a fossil garden on the school grounds, school administrators were open to other ministries—tutoring, twice-a-year delivery of goody packages to teachers to let them know they are appreciated, and being an advocate for the school with the local school board in resolving previously unresolved problems.

The following excerpt from a letter received from Buford and Jane Robinson of Morganton, North Carolina, shows the extent to which a church can network with community agencies and individuals outside their own congregation in an Operation Inasmuch.

One of the projects of Mission Morganton 2000 was a food distribution to low-income families. Particularly gratifying to us was the fact that our church members who participated in this project were not the only ones involved. In planning and directing the project, we involved others from the community:

- The project was done in conjunction with Burke United Christian Ministries, who made it possible to get food from the Metrolina Food Bank in Charlotte, N.C.
- A coordinator of Social Services and local church gave advice based on her involvement in an earlier food distribution that her church had sponsored.
- The city recreation center loaned some of their tables for us to use, delivering them and picking them up themselves.
- Two members of the Burke Literacy Council gave advice about where to advertise the upcoming food distribution.
- The Spanish Club teacher in a local middle school heard about the project from the Literacy Council and asked if her students could participate. She and her husband and two students worked with our church members during the actual distribution of food.
- The Literacy Council asked a Guatemalan lady who is a leader among some of the Hispanic [people] in

our community to assist, and she also worked with us that day.[5]

This leads to a second impact on the community. *Two, it enhances the church's image in the community.* Congregations that narrow their focus to traditional spiritual activities such as worship and Bible study are missing the opportunity to influence their communities. Their non-church-attending neighbors may well view them as "holy huddles," or exclusive enclaves of religious groupies. By commissioning their members to get involved in other local ministries or even secular helping agencies, they would enlarge their credibility manifold. They just might gain a hearing for the good news of God's love *if* they demonstrate it.

Several coordinators I interviewed indicated that they often receive favorable comments from persons from their community not associated with their congregations. Jim Everette of Ardmore Baptist Church, Winston-Salem, North Carolina, told me: "An elderly lady left a message this week that said: 'Mr. Everette, do you still have those missions days when you have people go out and make home repairs? If you do, would you call me because I sure do have some needs right now.'"[6] Violet Smith of Germanton, North Carolina, describes the new respect her church has from her community:

Our community has begun to realize that we are a church that is active and willing to help when there is a need. We were recently approached by a local school and asked to partner with them. Since we are a small community, we have no industry for them to ask. They said they had decided we were the most active organization in the community because of our Operation Inasmuch. A mother called recently and said that her child in another school needed tutoring and the school had suggested she call us to see if we could handle that, which we did. The Red Cross called recently to see if we would be willing to install smoke detectors in the homes of people who needed them. We find that when we tell people in the community that we go to Germanton Baptist Church, they say "You all are the ones who do so much for people, aren't you?" The next comment is usually, "That's what churches ought to be doing."[7]

A fresh story comes from the tenth anniversary of Operation Inasmuch, observed on April 16, 2005, in Fayetteville. Wayne Byrd, faithful volunteer in Operation Inasmuch, was helping to put a new roof on a home, one of about fifty such projects being conducted throughout the neighborhood. One could drive down the streets of the neighborhood and literally see work being done on every other house by churches of many different denominations.

Wayne got off the roof to get a drink of water. A woman who was walking down the street and talking on her cell phone called out to him, "Come here!" She asked him, "What's going on around here? What are all these white folks doing here?" He explained that it was Operation Inasuch, when churches from Fayetteville go into a neighborhood and repair homes for people who can't afford to do the work themselves. She said, "What's your name?" When he told her, she said, "I'm talking to my accountant. Here, tell him what y'all are doing!" Byrd explained to the man on the other end of the phone what was taking place in this neighborhood and handed the phone back to the woman. He then returned to the roof and resumed working. In a few minutes he heard the woman's voice again, but this time it was close by. She had climbed up on the roof and said, "I can't believe y'all are doing this! Can I help? Can I hand you something?" She wasn't dressed for roofing, but she was so impressed with the ministry taking place that she wanted to be part of it. Such is the impact on a community when churches get outside the walls of their buildings to do ministry in Jesus' name.

Three, Operation Inasmuch builds fellowship with other churches. The trend is that once a church does an Operation Inasmuch, other churches hear about it and want to know how they can become involved. Within three years, this ministry in Fayetteville went from one Baptist church fielding about 450 volunteers to a dozen or more churches putting as many as 1,500 volunteers to work in the community. I do not believe it is an exaggeration to say that Operation Inasmuch has done more to build bridges between faith systems in Fayetteville than any other single event. Consistently, the feedback is that congregations enjoy working with folk from other congregations. One church coordinator put it well:

> It's almost as if we don't have a comprehensive understanding of who God is until we join with other churches from different theological traditions. [And then] we're really able to embrace and begin to see the bigness and vastness of God. The nature of ministry is you can get in there and argue about theological differences or you can get in there and work cooperatively to put a roof on a house or to paint a community center or whatever. I think there is an active worship experience, almost a divineness that goes beyond language, to communicate the body of Christ by working in building the kingdom of God.[8]

As a Baptist, I am aware of the cloud of theological controversy that often overshadows relationships among sister congregations. Unfortunately, such controversies prevent these congregations from pooling their efforts to make a greater impact on their community. However, Operation Inasmuch has been demonstrated as an effective tool in just such collaborations. In the northeast region of North Carolina, as many as one hundred twenty Baptists congregations covering nine counties conducted an Operation Inasmuch on the national "Make a Difference" Day. Each Association, or local grouping of Baptist churches, focused on their own community, enlisted and trained CPR (Community Project Resource) Leaders, and recruited congregations to take whatever number of projects they felt they could manage. In some cases congregations worked solo, and in other cases they collaborated with each other to accomplish more. When asked if Operation Inasmuch is a good model to help strengthen relationships among congregations, Wendy Edwards, regional Baptist leader said: "Absolutely. We had congregations of every political and theological stripe working together."[9]

Operation Inasmuch also helps to build bridges among people of different races. The first occasion of sharing Operation Inasmuch with another church was when Snyder Memorial invited First Baptist Church of Fayetteville, an African American congregation, to participate with us. A team composed of members of both churches did the planning. Volunteers from both churches staffed each of the projects. It's not uncommon for congregations of differing races to worship together, but it is difficult for meaningful relationships to result from these joint experiences. On the other hand, working side by side all day long does it. At the end of the day, relationships had been established that continue to this day. As a result of this experience the two congregations have worshiped together more than once, and conducted a pilot project of racial reconciliation for the city.

One church has formed a partnership with a Hispanic congregation. In their first Operation Inasmuch the church went to the Hispanic church to help them make repairs on their modest place of worship. The following year their Hispanic friends asked if they could help with other projects in Operation Inasmuch. Another congregation planned their next Operation Inasmuch with an African American church in their community. The pastor wrote: "The bonds of fellowship are already being enjoyed as the two congregations plan a great day of witness through ministry that will surely honor the Lord."[10]

The stories in chapter 1 about the recognition Operation Inasmuch has received in Fayetteville evidence that the cross-cultural potential of this type of event is making itself known. Something about working alongside a person of a different race and culture facilitates genuine community. Roger Stancil of Fayetteville puts it this way:

> When churches come together—black churches, white churches, Korean churches, Chinese churches—it is a special opportunity. The more we broaden our

understanding of each other, the more we become a true community. That sounds very simple, but my experience is that people don't realize that until they have the opportunity to work together.[11]

Four, Operation Inasmuch helps to heal broken neighbor-hoods. Since many of the projects are concentrated in one neighborhood, impact on that neighborhood is maximized. Much more than home repair is accomplished; self-image is repaired, too. One nonprofit employee who qualifies families for Operation Inasmuch projects describes it this way:

> In a neighborhood off Sapona Road there is one happy little eight-year-old boy because there is no water pouring down into his bedroom this morning. His family has a new roof on their house. There is a seventy-eight-year-old widow who lives on less than $600 a month whose house isn't peeling and looking shabby anymore because she has a new paint job and a trim that's the prettiest hyacinth blue you've ever seen. There is an older couple who has decent plumbing for the first time in years, and a family of seven who has a home that will last a lot longer because all those old rotten boards and all that rotten siding is off their home. Those are just some of the…people who will never be the same because of Operation Inasmuch…Over the years most of these neighborhoods…have really felt forgotten, this one especially. But today they don't feel that way anymore because God's churches in this community made a promise and they kept it.[12]

Following this Operation Inasmuch, people from the local community college went into that same neighborhood with a literacy program. They usually have three or four people who avail themselves of this training, but on this occasion seventeen people came, largely because of what had taken place there a week before. The teachers said to those who arranged the

Operation Inasmuch: "You really opened up this neighborhood for us."[13]

This chapter began with a reference to a newspaper article detailing the impact of Operation Inasmuch on the community. Perhaps the best way to conclude it is to provide an excerpt from another article, since it comes from an objective observer. Robert Bell of *The Fayetteville Observer-Times* writes:

> To hear residents tell it, a battle of biblical proportions was waged Saturday throughout Massey Hill.
>
> On Progress Street, a young woman rocks on her front porch drinking deeply from a tall can of something in a brown paper bag. She sings loudly from a song drifting from somebody's window: "*I can love you better than she can.*"
>
> Farther up the street, a stranger to the neighborhood pushes hard on his broom, sweeping up all the bottles, bags, dust, and [debris] that have collected over the months.
>
> His associates run an orange extension cord up a rotted porch and through the front door to an electrical outlet.
>
> The juice triggers a circular saw. Hammers start to pound. The woman with the paper bag retreats, and her music shuts off. Operation Inasmuch has begun.
>
> In one of the city's oldest and occasionally dangerous neighborhoods, 15 Fayetteville churches united Saturday to make a difference for families building lives there.
>
> On Progress Street, Josephine Davis got a new roof and front porch, not to mention a testimony for her church today. "I'll be running up and down the aisles singing his praises," she said. "Couldn't be nothing but the Lord to make this happen."
>
> On Powell Street, neighbors Timothy Curtis and Wanda Johnson got some much-needed landscaping after volunteers cleared their overgrown yards of weeds and shrubs.

"It really looks nice," said Curtis. "Who would have thought?"

By day's end, two dozen houses were spruced up by Inasmuch volunteers, making for a lot of commotion and camaraderie in a neighborhood known more for its chaos.

Davis moved to the neighborhood in 1992 and has seen the community slide backward. "Some people around here don't want to take care of their homes, but a lot of folks like me can't afford it," said Davis.

When Inasmuch officials informed Davis earlier this year they would be fixing her leaky roof, she couldn't believe it. "My prayers were answered," she said.

Davis, a retired nursing assistant, sat in the living room of her small two-bedroom house while workers pounded on the roof. "I hope they pound all day," she said. "It's like music to my ears."[14]

Would that more churches were performing such music.

4

The Young and the Restless

There are times to be literal, and times to be figurative. It is time to get literal about human connectedness. The church has talked the language of interconnectedness, but it has been a sappy, figural connectivity. In its unveiling of the illusion of separateness, postmodern science is turning us into literalists about Jesus' words: "Inasmuch as you have done it unto the least of these, you have done it unto me."

LEONARD SWEET, *SOUL TSUNAMI*

At the beginning of the twenty-first century, every new programming idea or event for the church is evaluated in terms of its effectiveness for the younger generations of believers. Two facts motivate churches to do this. First, these are the church folk who are ascending to leadership in congregations, so any new idea must past muster with them. Second, every congregational leader is concerned about the decline in involvement in church activities by the youngest adults. Congregational leaders are looking for any help they can find to draw "Baby Busters" into their church life. Aware of this concern, I have included this chapter to show how Operation Inasmuch has unique appeal to "Busters." I have narrowed the focus of this chapter to Busters only because they are the generation that shows the least interest in religious activities and, therefore, pose the greatest challenges to involvement.

Who *Are* Those Guys?

One of my favorite lines comes from outlaws—Butch Cassidy and the Sundance Kid in the Robert Redford/Paul Newman flick of the same name from 1969. Having robbed a bank, they are fleeing from a posse, unaware that a famous Indian tracker leads the posse. They know only that none of their tricks of escape are working. Several times they look over their shoulders and say: "Who *are* those guys?" This is the question America has been asking about Baby Busters, and the one sociologists and theologians have been attempting to answer since the early 1990s.

Buster Turn-offs

Kevin Graham Ford provides an eye-opening look into the mindset of Busters in his book *Jesus for a New Generation*. He pulls no punches in describing the attitude of his peers toward traditional Christianity:

> My generation is not seeking out the church as an institutional gathering place where we can find comfort and an absolute moral authority. We don't care about theology. We don't care about denominational affiliation. We don't care about rites and liturgies and traditions. And we are turned off by hard-nosed doctrinal stands on nonessential issues—mode of baptism, charismatic gifts, women in ministry, and petty rules and attitudes about dress and lifestyle.[1]

The images Busters have of missions influence their willingness or lack thereof to get involved. Paul Borthwick identifies those images as

- shying away from cultural imperialism
- deep desire to work in partnership
- disdain for superiority
- diminished sense of the lostness of humanity[2]

For these and a host of other reasons we will see in this chapter, Busters pose a special challenge to congregational leaders at the point of involvement in mission causes. Yet as we will see, Operation Inasmuch is a fresh approach that holds particular promise in meeting this challenge.

Those between 20 and 40

Busters are Americans born between 1965 and 1983, which make them somewhere between about twenty and forty years old today. Their generation numbers sixty-six million people. They have been called Busters because their generation is smaller than the Baby Boomer generation, which includes 76 million people. They have received other labels:

- Thirteeners because they are the thirteenth generation of Americans
- Gen Xers from Douglas Copeland's 1991 novel
- Twentysomethings, although the older persons of this generation are already well into their thirties

Buster-shaping Events

One of the best ways of understanding Busters is to remember the events that have shaped their attitudes and worldview. In his book *Three Generations* Gary McIntosh[3] identifies these events:

Roe v. Wade—The Supreme Court decision in 1973 stating that the state could not restrict abortions during the first three months of pregnancy. This decision limited the number of babies born during this generation, thus its size.

High Technology—Busters are the first generation that cannot remember a time computers and other forms of technology were not part of everyday life. Using the language of cyberspace, futurist Leonard Sweet says: "My 22nd century kids are natives of the net. I am a naturalized citizen of the Net."[4]

The Challenger Disaster—The 1986 explosion of the space shuttle *Challenger* moments after takeoff had a similar effect on Busters that the assassinations of President Kennedy and Martin Luther King Jr. had on Boomers, and that the bombing of Pearl Harbor had on Builders.

Berlin Wall Dismantled—The November 1989 sudden destruction of the wall separating East from West Berlin symbolized the collapse of communism. Whereas older generations' worldviews were heavily influenced by the threats of communism, the youngest Busters have grown up in a different world.

Music—Any restraints that once existed in the production of popular music have disappeared, as the music of this generation is a no-holds-barred, max-volume explosion of sound and message.

Persian Gulf War—In stark contrast to Boomers' exposure to war—the fiasco of Vietnam—younger Busters were treated to an amazing feat of American military might and know-how, which has had predicable effects on such attitudes as patriotism and confidence in the military.

AIDS—At the same time attitudes about personal, sexual morality have relaxed, Busters have been confronted with the dangers of AIDS. "Never before has a generation been so aware of their own mortality."[5]

Clinton Administration—When Gary McIntosh wrote his book (1995), he admitted it was too early to know the effect of the first Baby Boomer President on the succeeding generation. We have a better idea now. Instead of inspiring as Kennedy's presidency did, Clinton's legacy is likely to create more cynicism in government and other established institutions as a result of the Lewinsky affair, among other things.

Buster Characteristics

These events have shaped Busters with a particular worldview and attitudes so as to pose a unique challenge to congregations wanting to involve them in the church. Before presenting how Operation Inasmuch helps meet that challenge, it is necessary to identify the characteristics of this special group. Perhaps Christian researcher George Barna has written the primer on Busters, *Baby Busters: The Disillusioned Generation.*[6] He describes Busters this way:

Busters are disillusioned—They feel alienated from life. They only trust personal experiences and have precious little hope for the future.

Busters feel abandoned—They are convinced they are getting a raw deal, saying: "We'll never be as well off as our parents." One Buster who is now a freelance futurist consulting for Christian congregations and denominations says: "We raised ourselves and each other," referring to his generation's growing up in a day-care and latch-key lifestyle.[7]

Busters want a high quality of life—They want it all, and they want it now. Quality of life means a "high fun quotient."

Busters are independent—They make their own decisions, often distrusting traditions or authority figures.

Busters are defensive—Since they are skeptical about having as many opportunities or possessions as their parents, they are protective of what they possess.

Busters are comfortable with change—"They grew up in the midst of chaos; they know nothing else. They are used to the fast pace and the lack of stability."[8]

Busters are more sensitive to people—They value building lasting relationships and showing sensitivity to people.

Busters are pluralists—They are tolerant of competing points of view. They embrace diversity.

Busters are flexible—They maintain a fluidity to life that facilitates change and openness to opportunities and new strategies.

Busters are pragmatic—"They are persuaded by what works, not what 'ought' to be."[9]

Taking the process of understanding Busters one more step, they value

- Relationships
- Fun
- Authenticity
- Experiences
- Results
- Real Change[10]

Here's the Ticket

At the risk of sounding overconfident, I am convinced Operation Inasmuch addresses most of the concerns and issues of Busters as indicated by these values and characteristics without compromising the integrity of the church's mission. Robert N. Nash Jr. makes a strong case for change in today's church to respond to the trends indicated in the attitudes of Busters and future generations.[11] In the beginning of his stimulating book he sets forth three primary responsibilities of the church:

- offer the truth of God's grace and love to its culture
- enhance the spirituality of its members
- cultivate a caring community that reflects the coming kingdom of God[12]

Operation Inasmuch does all these. It offers God's love and grace with hands-on ministry. It grows believers spiritually by helping them to experience biblical truth, as evidenced by the stories cited in chapter 2. Finally, it promotes a caring community that not only fosters authentic Christian fellowship within a given congregation, but also reaches out to the surrounding community in response to human hurts and hopes. If we are to understand that these are the goals of a congregation that is responsive to Busters, then by this test Operation Inasmuch can hardly be surpassed in its effectiveness at reaching and involving the young and the restless.

Allow me to make my case. Operation Inasmuch addresses five of the concerns or values of Busters.

Short-term commitment. As stated earlier, Busters are fluid in their approach to life. They are reluctant to make long-term commitments as evidenced by their hesitancy to establish membership in a church. Operation Inasmuch is a one-day event. It does not ask for long-term involvement. It is guerilla missions—responding to immediate needs and moving on to the next opportunity. Virtually every church coordinator of an Operation Inasmuch I spoke with in doing the research for this book listed the short-term aspect of it as one of its strongest appeals to younger members. This is the way one of them said it:

> One of the appeals of Operation Inasmuch is that it is time specific. Most of our Busters will not give you a week. They'll not give you a Saturday once a month for twelve months, but you let them know in advance and they'll give you a Saturday all day long going as hard as they can because they know they can go back to their family.[13]

Local focus. Busters have received a bum rap as being so self-centered that they are not willing to give their time to help others. The statistics say otherwise. As the following table shows, George Barna's research verifies that so far Busters are less involved in helping others than older generations; nevertheless, they are involved.

Activities in Which Busters Have Participated in the Last Thirty Days[14]

ACTIVITY	PARTICIPATION
went to a theater to watch a movie	78%
participated in corporate religion	55
were exposed to religious radio or television	44
volunteered time to help needy people in their area	44
discussed religious beliefs with someone of different belief	42
read a religious publication or book, other than the Bible	31
attended a class at a school or training center	30
volunteered time to help a non-profit organization or a church	27
avoided buying a specific product or brand because it was being boycotted by a cause or organization they support	21
volunteered time to help needy people in other countries	17

A closer look at Buster involvement reveals their strong preference for local concerns. Gary McIntosh asserts: "Busters want to make a difference in the world, but the causes they support are small *c* causes. More pragmatic than the generations before them, they want to be able to see the results of their involvement. Causes close to home attract their interest far more than national or worldwide causes."[15]

Operation Inasmuch suits the Buster preference for local, hands-on ministry. Of course, it is not unique in this regard. Other ministries meet this need as well, but the point I am making is Operation Inasmuch matches up well with the particular attitude of Busters to serve those who live closest to them. Paul Mundey, senior pastor of a large Brethren congregation in Maryland, says it well: "Mission is no longer 'over there' alone; it is also 'over here' in familiar and immediate neighborhoods. Such thinking translates into a new sort of church—a missionary church or congregation, I mean congregations engaging secular need 'up close and personal.'"[16]

Outward-directed. Despite the general feeling among Busters that they are not getting what they deserve, when they become involved in church activities, they expect those activities to be outward-directed. That is, they should focus on the needs of the community rather than the congregation or the needs of people in faraway places. Robert Nash says it this way: "...postmodern people want to know they are making a difference in their local communities. They want to participate in organizations that are working for change. They want to get their hands dirty. They want to see the visible results of their labors."[17]

This is the purpose of Operation Inasmuch—to get church folk outside the walls of their building to minister to people at their point of need. Once this purpose and plan are understood, people, including Busters, tend to respond easily. The match between value and event is so strong at this point that Gary McIntosh sounds like he is referring to Operation Inasmuch when he describes Busters' preference for an outward focus:

> If a church wishes to meet and reach the Busters of its community, it should become involved in community projects. Working together helps build trust between Christians and the Busters who get involved. Busters are often interested in projects having to do with kids from broken homes, homelessness, unemployment, and the environment. Your church might organize groups to paint the homes of elderly people or be big brothers and sisters, host a monthly birthday party, or provide tutoring or music lessons for needy children.[18]

Relationships. Busters feel isolated, touch-starved, and lonely. More than any previous generation, they are looking for meaningful relationships. Leonard Sweet says the dating service industry has doubled in size in the last seven years.[19] Technology is partly to blame. It has allowed, even encouraged, people to spend more time than ever alone in doing their jobs, being entertained over the Internet, even indulging in online spiritual activities instead of gathering with like-minded worshipers. As a result, the youngest of us, who are much more inclined to be high tech, are hungry for relationship.

Operation Inasmuch provides opportunities for Busters to interact with people from other generations. Again, feedback from churches that have conducted an Operation Inasmuch indicates that it does as much to foster a sense of belonging among participants as anything a church can offer. One coordinator in Greenville, North Carolina, said: "It was a good way to get the generations within our church to meet each other and work together—children and youth alongside median adults and senior citizens."[20] A young volunteer in another church said: "That's how I got started at this church. [Operation Inasmuch] was one of the first things I did. It was to get my feet wet. I did it for that reason—go get to know others."[21]

"HOT Missions"[22] is a term Leonard Sweet coined. It applies to Operation Inasmuch. HOT is an acrostic for high-online-technology and is his clever way of referring to Buster attitudes and behaviors. They do not want to be involved in something at a distance. They want personal, hands-on involvement. Sweet says HOT missions is "involvement in small, community-based initiatives." If he knew of Operation Inasmuch, perhaps he would include it along with Habitat for Humanity and Hospice as examples of mission activities that appeal to postmoderns.

An EPIC Ministry

Sweet argues persuasively for churches to take Busters' unique perspectives into consideration when developing ministries in which they expect Busters to participate. He gives four characteristics that *must* be true of such ministries if there is any hope for their success. They are expressed in the acrostic EPIC, which stands for Experiential, Participatory, Interactive, and Communal. Because these characteristics relate so well to Operation Inasmuch, it is worth the time and space to give some explanation of them here.

Experiential. Busters are looking for experiences. Their world promotes experiences. Sweet asks: "What does Planet Hollywood or Hard Rock Café deliver? Great food? They serve experiences."[23] An EPIC church is one that provides meaningful experiences for Busters because that is the best way of helping them understand what missions is about.

Participatory. Busters do not *need* participation; they *demand* it. I could not agree more with Sweet when he says: "It is now time to disestablish the clergy in the church once and for all. Postmodern culture is an 'age of participation,' an 'age of access'...The postmodern world is a karaoke world."[24] Writing about the changes required to reach Boomers and Busters for mission service, Ken Baker concludes that it will not come without offering a participatory leadership style in which missionary candidates are included in every level of decision-making.[25] EPIC congregations offer hands-on experiences to their members.

Interactive. Sweet blasts the refusal of churches to respond to new attitudes of the young when he says: "Our museums are doing better than our schools and churches in pioneering some of the best forms of interactivity out there."[26] Twentysomethings and thirtysomethings who are accustomed to interacting with video games, Internet chat rooms, and a host of other "interactivities" will not be content to "sit and soak" in church; they expect to be personally involved. An EPIC church empowers Busters to follow their sense of God's leading in doing ministry without loading them down with bureaucratic red tape. Again, the high-touch, participatory aspect of Operation Inasmuch makes it an especially good fit here.

Communal. Sweet cites the discovery of the United Methodist Church that people are wanting ministries that facilitate meaningful relationships. When Ezra Earl Jones, general secretary of the board of discipleship of that denomination, asked laity the question—"What works?"—the top five responses were: (1) Emmaus; (2) Disciple Bible Study; (3) Covenant Discipleship and other small group experiences; (4) VIM—Volunteers in Mission; (5) Camping. The common denominator in all these ministries is an emphasis on relationship. Note that volunteer missions is one of the top five of all effective church activities.

Elsewhere Sweet cites Walker Percy's definition of boredom: "the self stuffed with the self" as symptomatic of the absence of meaningful relationships of previous generations, which Busters wish to avoid. When churches learn how to unstuff people's lives with the things of self and replace them with things of God, they will have gotten back into the ballgame of competing for Busters' interest and involvement. Clearly, EPIC congregations understand their hunger for relationship and will offer plenty of opportunities for the same. Operation Inasmuch does this. I cite just one testimony:

> On the Sunday immediately following the first Operation Inasmuch, we had a dinner on the grounds, and we had a short program about what happened that day. There was an excitement we hadn't seen in a while. Operation Inasmuch is the one opportunity where we get all different age groups working together. Normally, folks are separated, but not in Operation Inasmuch. People got to know one another and helped to build a sense of family.[27]

If the reader cannot see already that Operation Inasmuch fits this paradigm perfectly, then I have done a poor job of relating its benefits in chapters 2 and 3. It touches all the bases—experiential, participatory, interactive, and communal. Or, to put it another way, it's an ecclesiastical home run! In doing research for this chapter I learned of a fellow pastor elsewhere in North Carolina who recently completed his doctoral dissertation on churches reaching Busters. Having been aware of Operation Inasmuch from a neighbor church, he cited it in his dissertation as one example of how congregations can do a better job of reaching the young and restless.

At the conclusion of his presentation of EPIC, Leonard Sweet asks a couple of poignant questions that should be applied to my claim that Operation Inasmuch is a Buster-type ministry. His questions are: "What shapes the life of your church—meetings or memories? Meetings issue forth more meetings. Only experiences issue forth the memories. Can you think of one meeting that promotes a more vital faith among your people?"[28] I have two file folders full of stories from people who vouch for the memory-making capacity of Operation Inasmuch. I will offer only one example.

> Raleigh King is a sixty-nine-year-old gentleman who attended the North Carolina School for the Deaf in Morganton. He has Ushers Syndrome and as a result is considered deaf and blind. Mr. King lives alone in a very rural part of Madison County, North Carolina. He has a sister nearby who takes him to the doctor and grocery store, etc. There is a small country gas station about a mile from his home. When he needs something, he walks to that store. The community has placed signs along the road that read: "Caution: Blind Man Walking."
>
> Raleigh is very independent. He rents the mobile home in which he lives. He is a great housekeeper. His bed is always made, his dishes washed, and everything is neat and orderly. He has a washer and dryer, and he does his own clothes. He maintains his own checking account. Raleigh has a stereo and television in his living room. The stereo can be heard from the driveway when you go to visit.
>
> During a recent Inasmuch, he was provided with a ramp and front porch with a roof. Raleigh enjoyed the interaction with the church group. He is patient with

anyone who does not know sign language. He communicates by printing in your palm. He takes great pride in educating others about deafness.

Mr. King tells us that he loves Jesus very much and that one day he will go to be in heaven with Him. He attends church in his community. The Inasmuch project along with a local agency have made it possible for Mr. King to stay in his home for a much longer period of time. The Inasmuch effort by Mars Hill Baptist Church did more than just provide access for Mr. King; it also gave him hope that he would be able to visit with his family, friends, and neighbors without fear of injury. Anyone who is privileged to know Mr. King has truly been blessed.[29]

I rest my case.

Making the Grade

*How wonderful that no one need wait a single moment
to improve the world.*

ANNE FRANK

*Life's most persistent and urgent question is "What are
you doing for others?"*

MARTIN LUTHER KING JR.

Have you ever had the experience of taking a test in school
on which you received a lower than expected grade because you
answered the wrong question? When our daughter was in college,
she phoned home upset because this very thing happened to
her. She had studied hard for the test and felt confident that she
had done well when she walked out of the classroom. But when
the professor handed her the graded exam, she had been given a
lower than expected grade. She had given complete answers
throughout the exam, but she had misunderstood one of the
questions. She had given good information, but it did not fit
the question on the test.

That is disconcerting when it happens with an important exam in college, but what if it were an even more significant test, say, the one that determines who is acceptable to the kingdom of God and who is not? You have no chance to "make it up" in that situation. What if the questions to that test were given in advance? Suppose you knew what will be asked of you when you face the final judgment? The failure to make the grade under those circumstances would be especially tragic, having the questions ahead of time and still giving the wrong answers!

In Matthew 25 Jesus gives the final exam for Kingdom faith. He tells us in advance what will be asked when the Judgment comes. We have no excuse for not knowing, for not making the grade. It's an open-book test.

In this chapter I want to explore some of the biblical teachings that support personal, hands-on, missions involvement such as Operation Inasmuch, specifically the teachings of Jesus. Any congregation or church leader contemplating the implementation of an Operation Inasmuch should be clear about the theological underpinnings of such an endeavor. We often rush too quickly to the "What?" of such an undertaking—how to do it—without giving adequate attention to the "Why?"— how this program helps us be the people of God in our time and place.

This is hardly an exhaustive survey of scriptural references to missions. Thick books have been written on that subject. Rather, I offer here a sampling of relevant passages to help the reader grasp the biblical basis for doing an Operation Inasmuch. Congregational leaders may find in this and the succeeding chapter help in motivating their people to get involved once an Operation Inasmuch has been scheduled and planned. Much of this material comes from messages I used as pastor in just that way.

Ministry Does It

Jesus says in Matthew 25 that the test of kingdom faith is ministry, specifically becoming involved in people's lives, responding to human hurts and hopes. Let it be noted up front that Jesus is setting forth the terms of eternity. The introductory verses make that plain—the Son of man coming in his glory, separating the sheep from the goats. Jesus says the determination of who gets into the Kingdom and who does not is on the basis of whether we have ministered to the needs of others.

That's not what people think, is it? Ask people whether they believe they are going to get into the kingdom of God, and they will often tell you they "hope so." They are likely to say something about being a good person (whatever that means) or being a church person or, if they are up on their theology, they may say they believe in Jesus. But Jesus does not have questions about any of these things on the final exam posed in Matthew 25. So, if these are our answers, we risk not making the grade.

When Jesus says the test of Kingdom faith is ministry, he is referring to feeding the hungry, being hospitable to strangers, clothing the naked, visiting the sick and imprisoned, and other such acts of compassion. These are the things he will want to know we have done when the time comes to determine whether our faith is sufficient to provide admission into the Kingdom. These are the questions on which we will be graded.

But what about John 3:16: "For God so loved the world that he gave his only Son, that whoever believes in him should not perish but have eternal life"? Evangelical Christians have long accepted this verse as the gospel in a nutshell, or the essence of what it means to be a believer—to believe in Jesus. Then how do we reconcile this call to simple faith with what Jesus says in Matthew 25? We do not need to reopen the grace versus works debate, which, as far as I am concerned, has been settled for a long time. We have been saved by grace to do good works. Or, to put it another way, we become followers of Jesus as a grace gift from the Father; we live as his follower by showing that grace to others, particularly in ministry to them at their points of need.

Two other passages shed light on this discussion as well. In the parable of the good Samaritan (Lk. 10:25–37) Jesus says a person keeps the commandment to love God and neighbor by ministering to a neighbor. When you read the context in which that parable was first given, you see that Jesus was responding to a question a lawyer asked about who his neighbor was. Like many of us, he was entangled in the interpretation of the commandment to love God and neighbor rather than focusing on its implementation. Jesus was always more interested in implementation than debate. His response in the form of one of the best-known stories in Western culture proves it.[1]

A New Testament passage that helps clarifies the relationship of belief with ministry is James 2:14–17:

> What does it profit, my brethren, if a man says he has faith but has not works? Can his faith save him? If a brother or sister is ill-clad and in lack of daily food, and one of you says to them, "Go in peace, be warmed and filled," without giving them the things needed for the body, what does it profit? So faith by itself, if it has no works, is dead.

This passage leaves little wiggle room. Belief *will* express itself in ministry. Authentic faith in Jesus *will* cause us to respond to human hurts and hopes as he did. Belief in Jesus is the first step toward Kingdom faith, but only the first step. Philip Yancey says: "A faith that does not drive me to the hurting and bleeding of humanity is a false faith."[2]

Such ministry cannot be done from a distance. Many a congregation has bought into checkbook missions, letting financial support of mission work, whether international or local, be their primary strategy for addressing the needs of others. This strategy is no longer adequate, if indeed it ever was. Operation Inasmuch challenges believers to get "up close and personal" with their involvement in missions.

A Trick Question

A trick question appears in the exam Jesus gives in Matthew 25. He says our ministry to others is in fact ministry to him.

Read the passage again with emphases I've added:

> "*I* was hungry and you gave *Me* food, *I* was thirsty and
> you gave *Me* drink, *I* was a stranger and you took *Me* in,
> *I* was naked and you clothed *Me*, *I* was sick and you
> visited *Me*, *I* was in prison and you came to *Me*." Then
> the righteous will answer Him, saying, "Lord, when did
> we see *You* hungry and feed *You*, or thirsty and give *You*
> drink? When did we see *You* a stranger and take *You* in,
> or naked and clothe *You*? Or when did we see *You* sick,
> or in prison, and come to *You*? And the King will answer
> them, "Assuredly, I say to you, *inasmuch as you did it to
> one of the least of these My brethren, you did it to Me.*"
> (NKJV)

So Jesus is testing us by how we minister to *him*! But how
do we minister to him? Who wouldn't minister to Jesus if they
had the chance? Who wouldn't do anything they could for Jesus
if they just knew how? But that's precisely the point. If Jesus
were to knock on our door and say, "I have not eaten for several
days," we'd fall all over ourselves to prepare the most sumptuous
meal imaginable for him, give him the honored place at our
table, and wait on him like a doting servant. But let a dirty,
homeless man knock on our door and see what we do. If Jesus
were to send word to us that he is lonely and afraid in prison,
we would not let the sun go down before we went to him and
took with us a beautiful picnic basket filled with all sorts of
goodies. But let a convicted criminal with a long record send
word that he is lonely and afraid, and we can find plenty of
reasons why we should not go. You see, Jesus is watching to see
whether we do for people simply because they have a need. He
is looking for sincere ministry, not showy ministry. Having the
exam ahead of time doesn't make it any easier to make the grade.
On this test, a passing grade is genuine, selfless caring.

Until we see our neighbors across the street or across the
tracks as persons with real needs, we will not be moved to get
out of our comfort zone to minister to them. This is why

Matthew 25:40 is the source of the name of Operation Inasmuch: We intend that its very name remind us constantly that we are ministering to Jesus himself when we do for others. We are encouraged that this point is actually sinking in.[3] In one of the workshops our church offered to help other churches learn how to do an Operation Inasmuch, one of our teenagers, Lindsey Comstock, was among those who shared testimonies of what their involvement has meant to them. She said something that captures the spirit of Jesus in Matthew 25: "God isn't looking for publicity, but a big heart and a willing hand."

Seeing Jesus

If, as I have suggested, Matthew 25 is a test of Kingdom faith, then the key to making the grade is the ability to recognize Jesus when we see him. We can miss him if we are not alert. After all, he will not appear to us with a halo over his head looking like the picture in your grandmother's house—soft, brown eyes, long, black hair, and a full beard. He is not about to walk up to us and say, "Shalom. I'm Jesus of Nazareth. Want to see a miracle?" He's not that obvious and noticeable, but he *is* here.

He is the abused wife who dreads to hear her alcoholic husband come home at night because she doesn't know whether she will get through the night without a beating. He is the misfit teenager who does not know how it feels to be accepted by his peers, who would rather take a beating than go to school where he is ridiculed and persecuted unmercifully. He is the wealthy woman who has always had anything she wants in the way of material things but yearns for the one thing she does not have— real friends who accept her for herself, not because of her money. He is the pregnant teenager who is scared and lonely and confused, who wants to do the right thing about her baby but wonders if she can, if she can provide a decent home for the child when it is born and wonders if she has just sealed her fate for the rest of her life. He is the homeless man pushing a shopping cart with all his worldly possessions, sleeping in the woods, under overpasses, and in cardboard boxes, taking meals at the Salvation Army or wherever he can find them. Jesus is, dare I say it, the AIDS patient who is cut off from everyone because they are afraid of him, who is dying with hardly anyone to comfort him.

If I understand Matthew 25, Jesus is most definitely all of these persons and a multitude of other hurting people. But we seldom recognize him. He is here, but we do not see him.

Francis of Assisi saw him. Not for a long time, for Francis was a wealthy young man, highborn and high-spirited, but he was not happy. He felt his life was not complete. One day when he was out riding, he met a leper, loathsome and repulsive in the ugliness of his disease. Something moved Francis to dismount and fling his arms around this wretched sufferer, and in his arms the face of the leper changed to the face of Jesus.

In a more contemporary scene, worshipers were gathering for Sunday morning services when they were confronted with something they had never seen before—a homeless man on the sidewalk leading up to the sanctuary. He said nothing to the finely dressed saints but sat there wrapped up in a dirty blanket. In a way reminiscent of the passersby in the parable of the good Samaritan, they moved quickly by the homeless man. After all, if they stopped to talk to him, they might be late for church.

When the worship service began, the pastor was not in his usual place. The congregation hardly noticed at first, but as the service went on, they became more and more curious as to where the pastor was and who was going to deliver the sermon. Imagine how shocked they were when the time for the sermon came and a dirty, ill-clad, homeless man—the same one who had been sitting out front—entered by a side door and walked up to the pulpit. He took off the filthy baseball hat and removed the fake beard. It was the pastor! He didn't have to say much that day. The sermon had already been acted out. It wasn't Jesus who appeared to that stunned congregation, but they could hardly miss the point of Matthew 25 in their pastor's courageous portrayal. Ministry to hurting people is ministry to Jesus. And such ministry is not an option for a New Testament church.

Operation Inasmuch provides an effective way to get more church folk involved in this kind of ministry, thereby making the grade on Jesus' test in Matthew 25.

The reader should be clear about the relationship of ministry to salvation. What we have said here about ministry is to be balanced with other teachings of Jesus on the priority of believing in him. But, of course, the point is: True belief will lead to action. Going beyond *mere belief* leads into another of Jesus' teachings.

Growing beyond the Minimum

Another teaching of Jesus that contributes to the theology of Operation Inasmuch comes from his encounter with the rich, young man. This story also speaks to the relationship of belief and action as discussed earlier. Luke has preserved it for us:

> And a ruler asked him, "Good Teacher, what shall I do to inherit eternal life?" And Jesus said to him, "Why do you call me good? No one is good but God alone. You know the commandments: 'Do not commit adultery, Do not kill, Do not steal, Do not bear false witness, Honor your father and mother.'" And he said, "All these I have observed from my youth." And when Jesus heard it, he said to him, "One thing you still lack. Sell all that you have and distribute to the poor, and you will have treasure in heaven; and come, follow me." But when he heard this, he became sad, for he was very rich. (Lk. 18:18–23)

One of the things Jesus did was stir the yearnings for deeper spiritual experiences in many who heard him. As they listened to the carpenter-turned-teacher, their frustrations with the legalism and coldness of Judaism as it was practiced in the first century were exposed to the full light of God's truth. Listening to the simple, straightforward truths Jesus spoke, and watching him reach out to all kinds of people in love and compassion was like looking for the first time through a window that had been cleaned from years of dirt and grime. This is one reason the masses were drawn to him—not just because he put on a good show with many miracles, but because he connected with something deep inside them that said, "There has to be something more to faith than keeping laws and observing rituals."

One of the people who came to Jesus for this reason was an official of a local synagogue. Contrary to the opinion of some, I believe he was a sincere young man. Nothing indicates that he was like others who tried to trap Jesus with trick questions. Rather, he came honestly looking for something. Perhaps it was little more than confirmation that he was on the right track already, but his was an honest inquiry.

We are not told much about this young man. Luke says he was religious. He had a sterling record of maintaining the strict Jewish laws. When Jesus reminded him of the usual Jewish terms of righteousness—keeping the commandments—this man was faithful in every way. We can conclude, then, that he was not casual about his faith. He was not given to compromise. Yet, he was not satisfied. Apparently, he came to Jesus because his religiosity was not enough. He was haunted by the thought that there could be something more—more satisfying, more joyful, more meaningful.

Most church folk can identify with the thoughts that moved this young man to look up Jesus. They go through the motions of practicing their faith as they believe they should, but it's not enough. Just attending church is not enough. Serving on a committee or two is not enough. Depending on the pastor or other professional ministers to provide spiritual nourishment is not enough. There has to be something more.

Of course, not everyone experiences this inward yearning. Every congregational leader struggles to understand the diversity of commitment in his or her congregation, and this struggle often leads to categorizing the various levels of commitment. I offer my own here. It seems to me that we have four kinds of church folk. First are the *people of habit*. These are the folk for whom church is more custom than commitment. Religion is more cultural than personal. Through years of thoughtless participation, faith has become second nature. Church has become a spectator event. The idea that faith might have something more to it than sitting through a worship service and perhaps a Bible study class has never occurred to these people. They have little or no motivation to grow or deepen a shallow faith. What they have is quite enough for them, thank you.

On the other end of the spectrum are the *happy Christians*. The church is the center of their social life as well as their religious life. These are the most mature and active of all the people in the church. Even so, they are eager to grow. They are never satisfied with the status quo. They find spiritual activities meaningful and stimulating. They are the first to volunteer almost any time a plea goes out for help with anything around the church, and they will be the front line team in any Operation Inasmuch.

A third type of church folk is what I call *trapeze Christians*. These people have some understanding of Christian commitment but believe they can balance it with other self-interests. They want to have their cake and eat it, too. They want to be faithful but have a hard time pulling away from other interests, so they teeter precariously on the high wire of compromise between success in a materialistic, hedonistic culture and humble, steady commitment to the Lord of lords.

The fourth type is *good citizen Christians*. They want the church to do well. They are committed to a point, but their motivation is the success of the institution. They are willing to serve the church, especially if they are convinced their service will advance the popularity of the church in the community. They are often frustrated with their faith. Their spiritual experiences have been meaningful but not long lasting.

People from these last two groups—trapeze and good citizen Christians—are the ones who will benefit the most from a personal, hands-on experience in mission work. They are the folk who occasionally feel the yearning for something more, as did the young man of Luke 18. I am convinced this yearning is the work of God's Spirit, who does not settle for mediocrity, but presses for excellence. The Spirit is like a coach who pushes players to be the best they can be, or like a military commander who knows the dangers of complacency when it comes to soldiering. God's Spirit prompts us to look for the something more that we need.

If God's Spirit prompted him to approach Jesus, the young man in Luke 18 did not hear what he hoped to hear. Initially, he did. When he asked Jesus what he had to do to have eternal life, Jesus reminded him of the Jewish way to righteousness: Obey the commandments. To this the young man quickly and proudly replied: "All these I have observed from my youth."

But at that point the conversation took an unexpected turn. Jesus told him he lacked one thing yet: He should sell all his stuff and give the money to the poor.

Here interpretations of this story normally focus on the problems of wealth. Luke says the young man left Jesus disappointed because he was a rich man. Implication: He valued his possessions more than he valued the something more he came to Jesus to find. Certainly, Jesus used this incident to warn his followers about the dangers of wealth. Riches can blind a person to the truth. They can become insurmountable barriers to one's entrance into the Kingdom.

Let's look beyond these usual and obvious interpretations of what Jesus said to the young man. Jesus told him to sell his things and *give the money to the poor*. He told him to do something good for people who had less than he did. He told him to take a stand for the disadvantaged. A good case can be made for interpreting Jesus' teaching in this story to say that the something more the young man came looking for was doing for others.

My point is this: Ministry to others is one of the best ways of developing a more effective Christian life. Faith grows best when expressed in behavior. The story of the "rich young ruler," as he is called, suggests that doing for others both grows our faith and qualifies us to be named among Jesus' followers. Doing for others is more than praying for them or giving money to support programs to help them. There comes a time when we have to roll up our sleeves and get personally involved in their lives.

It's like giving to a special fund-raising campaign. We give our tithe or at least a usual amount week after week, month after month, all year long to help the church pay her bills. However, every once in a while a need comes along, usually a capital project of some kind, that requires us to do more, to give over and above our regular giving. Mark it down! This is the giving that brings the most satisfaction. It costs more, but it makes us feel better to do it. It may even force us to do without something but we don't mind because we receive something better in return—a deep, inner peace and joy that we get only when love moves and motivates us.

Several years ago, I went with a team of volunteers from my church on an evangelistic mission trip to Venezuela. One of my assignments for the week was to preach in evangelistic services in the Baptist church in the city of Barquisimeto. The week was half gone before I realized that it was the first time I had preached without any expectation of compensation. I had preached outside my own pulpit before, but always with the assumption (without any prior agreement) that there would be some honorarium. Not so with my preaching in Barquisimeto. Not only did I not expect to be paid to preach, I paid my own expenses to go there to proclaim the gospel. That was one of the most fulfilling experiences in preaching I've ever had.

The same was true for more recent experiences in Zambia and South Africa. It was tough going—speaking through an interpreter, constantly weighing what I said to allow for differences between my own culture and that of my hearers—but it was pure joy. I account for that fact by recognizing it was over-and-above ministry, not as duty or in fulfillment of a job description, but reaching beyond the minimum.

This is what Operation Inasmuch is about—providing ways for ordinary church folk to discover the deeper satisfaction of personal ministry to others. And the testimonies of participants validate this claim.

"Even So Send I You"

No examination of Jesus' teachings in support of hands-on involvement in mission work is complete without remembering his commissioning of the disciples following his resurrection. Matthew's version is better known and probably more complete, but I like John's because it's so succinct: "As the Father has sent me, even so I send you" (Jn. 20:21).

This is the church's commission. God sent Jesus; now Jesus sends his followers. These are our marching orders, our mission and reason for being. The most important parts of speech in this brief commission are the conjunctions—"as" and "even so." They show a connection between the sending of Jesus into the world and the sending of his followers into that same world. We are to go in the same way and for the same reasons he came. We are to carry on what he began.

The key to understanding Jesus' meaning in John 20:21 is his first sermon given in the synagogue in his hometown of Nazareth. There he laid out the platform of his ministry. On that occasion he applied the prophecy of Isaiah 61:1–2 to himself:

> The Spirit of the Lord is upon me,
> because he has anointed me to preach good news
>   to the poor.
> He has sent me to proclaim release to the captives
> and recovering of sight to the blind,
> to set at liberty those who are oppressed,
> to proclaim the acceptable year of the Lord.
> (Lk. 4:18–19)

Few churches today contain the kinds of folk to whom Jesus came to minister. We don't meet many "captives" or "blind" or "oppressed" in the church, so it is necessary to go outside the walls of the church to find them. Ministering to them is not an option; it's *assumed* (that is, if we go out as Jesus did). And personal, hands-on mission work in our own community is ministry at its best.

In his book *The Biblical Basis of Missions*, Avery Willis has identified the two leading misconceptions regarding mission work: One, that missions is only for a few extraordinary people, and two, that missions can be done by proxy.[4] He elaborates: "Missions by proxy is the standard operating procedure for many churches...Some Christians interpret their giving as paying their part of missions gifts and thereby discharging their obligations to evangelize the world."[5]

These ways of thinking about missions do not take into account Jesus' sending of his followers after the resurrection. Either they unnecessarily narrow the focus of Jesus' statement to apply only to those who are called into vocational missions, or they infer by his words that being once or twice removed from actual mission work is acceptable as long as one is at least supportive. But these are unfortunate distortions of Jesus' meaning. What he says in John 20 applies to *all* his followers.

Fortunately, we have good reason to think these misconceptions are fading. The rapid spread of Operation Inasmuch indicates that churches and individual believers are embracing the hands-on approach to missions. Whether they see the connection between Jesus' commissioning in John 20 and their own ministry, or they simply prefer local mission work to global efforts, is something that would have to be settled on a case-by-case basis. But the connection is there—understood or not.

Jesus said it: "As the Father has sent me, even so I send you." It's up to us to do it. Making the grade as mature, Kingdom-building, eternity-bound Christians depends on our doing it.

6

This Is the Church

Remember that when you leave this earth, you can take with you nothing that you have received—only what you have given: a full heart, enriched by honest service, love, sacrifice, and courage.

SAINT FRANCIS OF ASSISI

It is not how much you do, but how much love you put in the doing.

MOTHER TERESA

Hands-on mission work in local communities is nothing new. It has taken place since the beginning of the church, but it often has to overcome the inertia of institutionalism to do so. When it does, it can redefine what it means to do church.

A church in Florida began a ministry of meeting needs in its own community. Church members gave their Sunday afternoons to do what they could to touch people at their points of need. One group bought groceries and cooked dinner for the local Salvation Army shelter. Along with physical food, they gave out spiritual food in the form of New Testaments to the people they served. Another group visited a local children's hospital, ministering to the children and their parents in any way they could. Linda, a nurse in the church, was involved in this ministry. One Sunday afternoon she visited a ten-year-old boy and his father. The father was a pastor in the area. During the visit he said to Linda, "This is Sunday; shouldn't you be in church?" Linda said, "Sir, this is church."[1]

How does a congregation get to that level of understanding about the mission of the church? What has to happen for church folk to break out of the consumer mentality that keeps them imprisoned inside the walls of the church house, and begin to see themselves as missionaries in their own community?

The short answer is: The Bible can do it. The more believers understand the biblical concepts of what it means to be the people of God, the more they will be driven beyond the walls of the church buildings to minister to their neighbors. In the previous chapter I explored some of Jesus' teachings that speak to personal, hands-on mission work, but that is not the full story. The entire biblical witness in one way or another challenges believers to be other-focused, that is, to influence their world for God, and that clearly begins in their own community. Learning from a variety of characters, we now expand our examination of the "Why?" of Operation Inasmuch.

Are We Listening?

Doing hands-on, volunteer mission work is a matter of listening to the right voice. Many voices speak in, to, and through the church. The *voice of statistics* ever sings the tunes of that famous trio: "The Three Bs" (buildings, baptisms, and budget). Denominations are eager to give this trio center stage with their preoccupation with the statistics of institutionalism. Personal ambitions of climbing the career ladder make congregational leaders vulnerable to the seductions of this particular voice.

The voice of fellowship calls us to "take care of our own." Fellowship is an important aspect of church life. No congregation can be healthy without it. But if it is given too much emphasis, the church can become inward-focused, to the neglect of those outside the fellowship. The fellowship voice can make hearing the voice of God calling the church outside her walls more difficult. One pastor whose church has conducted more than one Operation Inasmuch told me that the major obstacle they faced was the feeling of some in his congregation that they ought to be helping their own members before helping others. The fellowship voice was especially loud in that church.

Akin to the fellowship voice is *the sanctuary voice.* I do not mean one that is heard in the church's worship center, but one that calls for the church to be a sanctuary or safe place for Christians. Perhaps you are aware of the school of thought that says Christians should resist the lures of worldliness and ungodliness by withdrawing into their safe communities. They should promote their own values by limiting their contact with unbelievers as much as possible. At the risk of oversimplification, I am willing to suggest that this line of thinking is one reason for the multiplicity of Christian schools, Christian Yellow Pages, and the like. I have no quarrel with the idea that believers are to live a distinctively Christian lifestyle that will inevitably put us at odds with a culture that is unfriendly, and sometimes hostile, to Christian values. But I do not believe Jesus meant for his followers to withdraw from the world. His statement, "As the Father has sent me, even so I send you," examined in the previous chapter is incontrovertible evidence for that fact. Though well-intentioned, the sanctuary voice can make it hard to hear the voice of God calling His people to get out into the world and be His hands, feet, and voice to those who need Him.

We can learn to listen to the right voice from the experience of Samuel. His mother, Hannah, brought him as an infant to the Hebrews' holy place in fulfillment of her promise that if God would give her a son, she would give him to the Lord.

When Samuel was old enough to understand, God called him:

> Now the boy Samuel was ministering to the LORD under
> Eli. And the word of the Lord was rare in those days;
> there was no frequent vision.
>
> At that time Eli, whose eyesight had begun to grow
> dim, so that he could not see, was lying down in his
> own place; the lamp of God had not yet gone out, and
> Samuel was lying down within the temple of the LORD,
> where the ark of God was. Then the LORD called,
> "Samuel! Samuel!" and he said, "Here I am!" and ran to
> Eli, and said, "Here I am, for you called me." But he
> said, "I did not call; lie down again." So he went and lay
> down. And the LORD called again, "Samuel!" And
> Samuel arose and went to Eli, and said, "Here I am, for
> you called me." But he said, "I did not call, my son; lie
> down again." Now Samuel did not yet know the LORD,
> and the word of the LORD had not yet been revealed to
> him. And the LORD called Samuel again the third time.
> And he arose and went to Eli, and said, "Here I am, for
> you called me." Then Eli perceived that the LORD was
> calling the boy. Therefore Eli said to Samuel, "Go, lie
> down, and if he calls you, you shall say, 'Speak, LORD,
> for thy servant hears.'" So Samuel went and lay down in
> his place.
>
> And the LORD came and stood forth, calling as at
> other times, "Samuel! Samuel!" And Samuel said, "Speak,
> for thy servant hears." (1 Sam. 3:1–10)

The mistake most people make when they read this familiar
story is to assume it was a unique experience for a special person
and not for ordinary folk such as occupy the pews on Sundays.
I grant you that Samuel's role in Israel was hardly ordinary. God
does not often call in an audible voice, but that does not mean
that He is recruiting for the Marines—only looking for a few
good men. What I am referring to here is one's availability, the

understanding that God can and wants to use anyone who is available to help alleviate human hurts and restore human hopes. Such an availability comes from hearing the sending voice of God. God's call as it came to Samuel is normative for all believers, but they seldom hear that voice above the cacophony of voices in the church.

A seminar on lay ministry was advertised with a headline that read: "THESE MEN REFUSED TO ACCEPT RESPON-SIBILITY." Underneath the line were pictures of St. Francis, Martin Luther, John Wesley, Alexander Campbell, John Mott, and Pope John XIII. "The point of the ad was simple," explain Gordon Loux and Ronald Wilson, "the word of the church must be shared, and all God's people are called to serve."[2]

The theology of this conviction is inherent in the doctrine of the priesthood of all believers. Every believer is empowered to speak for God, to bridge the chasm between unbelievers and God himself, to flesh out the truth of God in such a way as to help others believe. Says the New Testament to the church: "You are a chosen race, a royal priesthood, a holy nation, God's own people, that you may declare the wonderful deeds of him who called you out of darkness into his marvelous light" (1 Pet. 2:9). In light of this seminal verse, God's call to Samuel is valid for everyone who claims to believe in Jesus Christ. And if that's so, then I ask again: Are we listening?

On April 14, 1912, the ocean liner *Californian* had progressed to within fifteen hundred miles of Boston in the Atlantic Ocean. The officer on watch in the middle of the night spotted another steamer several miles away. He attempted to communicate by Morse code using the ship's beacon lamp, but he received no response. Through binoculars the officer watched a series of flashing lights near the steamer for about two hours. Finally, the lights stopped. They seemed to vanish in the night.

It was only coincidence that the lights had been seen at all. The *Californian* had reversed engines and parked because of the danger posed by an immense field of oceanic ice. That unscheduled stop had given the *Californian* a ringside seat for a historic drama. The distant ship had intended the lights, actually rocket flares, as distress signals. The *Californian* was only nine miles away and could have rushed to her aid. It was later learned that the unidentified ship was also sending distress signals by radio. The *Californian* was well within range of those messages, but her radio operator was asleep. That night the ship's second officer, from his vantage point of the bridge, unwittingly watched the sinking of the *Titanic*.

Before a congregation is willing to undertake an Operation Inasmuch they, or at least their leaders, must hear the voice of God above the noise of the world and of the competing voices in the church. They must recognize God's voice, as Samuel eventually did, and listen to God's instructions to get personally involved in ministry to a desperate world.

Vision Makes the Difference

One reason some Christians are not able to hear God's call is they lack vision. This is often rightfully said of congregations. It also applies to individual believers. They do not see the big picture of what God wants to do. Their vision is myopic, focused only on church work and unable to see the work of the church. The apostle Paul can inspire such persons to broaden their vision.

One experience made a difference in his life and in the kingdom of God—his vision of a call from Macedonia. Luke reports it this way:

> And a vision appeared to Paul in the night: a man of Macedonia was standing beseeching him and saying, "Come over to Macedonia and help us." And when he had seen the vision, immediately we sought to go on into Macedonia, concluding that God had called us to preach the gospel to them." (Acts 16:9–10)

What does Luke mean by *vision* in this passage? The Bible drops in the word *vision* here and there as if we know what it means, but we really do not know. If it means Paul dreamed about going to Macedonia, we understand. We can identify with that kind of experience. But if it means God spoke to Paul through his subconscious mind, we are not so clear.

We all have dreams, but we do not all have visions. Dreams are our personal, private hopes—of being a pro basketball player, of one day having an idyllic cabin in the mountains, and so on. These are the aspirations of our youth, the projections of an idealistic mind, and, sometimes, an unrealistic appraisal of our own abilities. As often as not, these dreams are materialistic and self-centered.

Visions, on the other hand, are dreams that are other-focused. They are aimed outward. They find their fulfillment in the benefit of others, such as a doctor's vision of finding a cure for cancer, or a teacher's vision of unlocking the secret to learning for her students. Vision is what makes life exciting. It's what pushes a person not to settle for mediocrity, but to strive for excellence. When Helen Keller was asked if there was anything she could think of that was worse than being blind, she answered, "Yes! Being able to see and having no vision."[3]

Paul had such vision. Once again, however, the temptation to treat Paul's experience as a totally unique event, unavailable to ordinary Christians, is almost overwhelming. But I am convinced that Paul's response to the call from Macedonia came from his commitment to a greater vision that was not dependent on supernatural visions. His vision of missions was larger than any one city or country. That vision was to see the gospel preached as far as possible and to do whatever he could to see that happen. That vision, not the one reported in Acts 16, led to his departure for Macedonia. If he had not been open to go wherever God directed and do whatever God wanted him to do, he might never have understood the call from Macedonia.

The point I am making here is that a vision of missions that is big enough is likely to keep any believer open to opportunities to minister. If it worked for Paul, it can work for us. Consider the experience of Kathy Evans of Valparaiso, Indiana.

The leaders of her church said: "We need to be about our Father's business." "I'm business-minded," she said, "so I began to ask the Lord to show me what that meant. What is your business, Lord? What's close to your heart? And in a short time he began to bring into my life people who needed help in a lot of areas.

"I remember one morning I had prayed, 'Lord, I believe there is someone in Valparaiso who needs my help. Please show me that one.'

"Later that day I was shopping, and my kids insisted we eat at K-Mart. After I thanked the Lord for the food, I noticed that an elderly lady was watching us, and, in fact, seemed quite undone by what I'd done. As she left her table and passed by us, I nodded and smiled a greeting.

"Later, outside the store, I saw her waiting for a bus and struck up a conversation with her. It turned out that she was a very lonely woman. When I asked her if I could visit her, she said, 'Yes! And please bring the children.' It also turned out that she had cancer, and in the four months before she died, I was able to minister to her in several ways. I believe it came about because I asked the Lord to open my eyes to need. If we do that, we can expect him to show us."[4]

What if congregations were to see their communities as someone who does not live there sees them? What if we were to cancel worship services one Sunday and walk or ride around in our communities, taking note of the human hurts we see? Or better yet, surveying our communities to discover the needs that are there but are hidden? What difference would that make on how we spend our time and money?

One volunteer tells of the time his attitude about his community and working with others to improve it changed. He heard his pastor issue a moving challenge for his congregation to get involved in Operation Inasmuch. He read Matthew 25:40

with his own special inflection and emphasis. Jimmie Mitchell responded. He says:

> I began to envision what this program was really about. The work was to be done at Windsor Terrace [public housing]. We gathered at the big oak tree at the corner. Prayer was offered, and I saw people, God's people, all in one accord. I saw hearts and hands; old hands, young hands, large hands, small hands, all blessed by the power of God…doing what the Lord has commanded us to do. I saw no color, just God's people. I thought to myself, "Why can't we make Operation Inasmuch a daily venture in our lives?" That particular year my attitude changed so much.[5]

This is what a biblical vision of missions can do. It opens us to the possibility of being used by God in any given situation at any time. In my community, hundreds of soldiers live in a constant state of alert. They are subject to being sent anywhere in the world on a moment's notice. They have often been deployed so quickly that they were not able to let their families know they were going. They have had to wait until later to send word of their deployment, without any specifics of where they were or how long they would be gone. What if Christians adopted that posture with mission work? Some do, but not enough. Any congregational leader wanting to see his or her fellow believers embrace opportunities to minister outside the church's walls will be wise to cultivate a biblical vision in them. A vision such as that of the apostle Paul and Kathy Evans and Jimmie Mitchell will position a congregation to undertake an Operation Inasmuch with enthusiasm.

Saved for What?

Surely, any examination of the biblical witness to mission work includes the call of Isaiah. In response to a heart-stopping appearance of God, he said, "Here am I, send me." But look at the whole story:

In the year that King Uzziah died I saw the Lord sitting upon a throne, high and lifted up; and his train filled the temple. Above him stood the seraphim; each had six wings: with two he covered his face, and with two he covered his feet, and with two he flew. And one called to another and said:

"Holy, holy, holy is the LORD of hosts; the whole earth is full of his glory."

And the foundations of the thresholds shook at the voice of him who called, and the house was filled with smoke. And I said, "Woe is me! For I am lost; for I am a man of unclean lips, and I dwell in the midst of a people of unclean lips; for my eyes have seen the King, the LORD of hosts!"

Then flew one of the seraphim to me, having in his hand a burning coal which he had taken with tongs from the altar. And he touched my mouth, and said: "Behold, this has touched your lips; your guilt is taken away, and your sin forgiven." And I heard the voice of the Lord saying, "Whom shall I send, and who will go for us?" Then I said, "Here am I! Send me." (Isa. 6:1–8)

It is easy to become enamored of the mysterious and spectacular appearance of God to the prophet and miss its application to the basis of mission work. Notice that Isaiah's sinfulness was exposed instantly when he found himself in God's presence. To say that he felt unworthy would be an understatement of grand proportions. God's response was forgiveness. The scene here is vivid—touching his lips with a hot coal from the altar of the temple and pronouncing him forgiven. In an instant Isaiah was transformed from sin-sick to healed, from humiliated and broken to honored and whole.

Before we become too taken with the miracle of forgiveness, look what else happened to Isaiah. At once he heard God call: "Whom shall I send? Who will go for us?" Before Isaiah knew it, he blurted out: "I'll go! Send me!" With that enthusiastic response Isaiah was commissioned to a life of over-and-above service for the forgiving God.

Isaiah's experience illustrates the relationship between salvation and service. As soon as he was forgiven of his sin, Isaiah was called into service. It is impossible to overstate the importance of this relationship to hands-on mission work. The two are inextricably connected. Salvation leads to service as a college education leads to employment (or should). Isaiah understood his life work as a direct result of his encounter with God's grace. When grace is allowed to penetrate deep into our souls, we are naturally led to serve. This is not something that has to be taught or motivated. We must simply keep the terms of our salvation before us.

One of my favorite sayings comes from a gifted African American preacher, J. Alfred Smith. I once heard him preach at a conference where he was waxing eloquently regarding authentic Christian service. It wasn't what he said, but how he said it: "Jesus gave you not a title but a towel."[6] I have referred to that statement so often that one of my sisters did a cross-stitch of it and it hangs on my office wall. That says it as well as anything I know. Jesus did not pin a badge on our chest when we became one of his followers; he handed us a towel and showed us the dirty feet of our neighbors.

Allow me to be direct. Why do you think you have been forgiven? What did God have in mind in extending to you that gift of all gifts? Was it so you could feel superior to your unforgiven neighbors? Or was it so you could identify with the brokenness of those who live without God's love and then show them how to find wholeness? Was it merely to give you a sense of security about eternity? Or was it to call you to act as a guide for others to find the way? If you are like Isaiah, you understand that such a gift is not received without responsibility.

The motion picture *The Mission* of the late 1980s, starring Robert DiNiro, makes this very point. The story takes place during the colonization of South America by Europeans. In the story DiNiro plays a Portuguese man who becomes involved in a fight with his brother and kills him. Immediately, he is plunged into deep, deep grief and guilt. He is completely distraught and helpless. Eventually the church tells him that he must pay a heavy restitution for his sin.

Now this man is known widely for his mistreatment of the native people. He has enslaved them and abused them unmercifully. He has even gone beyond the territory allowed to carry on his illegal operations. So his restitution is to assist the church in a mission expedition deep into the jungle, into the same territory where the natives hate him. He is ordered to carry a huge net with his old soldier's armor on his back.

Quietly, but with great struggle, this man makes his way through the dense jungle with his burden on his back. They climb incredibly steep cliffs, cross deep rivers, and slash their way through places some animals couldn't go. When at last the expedition arrives at their destination, this man is nearly spent. He has climbed the last mountain, but he does not have enough strength left to pull his armor with him. He tries in vain several times to pull the armor up the hill behind him. He has come so far. Will he fail now? Will he get this close and no closer to paying his debt?

The Indians have been watching him for some time. They know nothing of why this man is pulling on the large net loaded with armor, but they can see his pitiful state, and they laugh at him. This soldier who has pilfered their villages and enslaved their people is a pathetic ball of humanity, and laughter is sweet revenge. With this man on his knees in utter exhaustion and shame, one of the Indians walks toward him with a knife. Justice would have him thrust the knife into his enemy's body. Instead, the Indian reaches behind the humiliated soldier and cuts the rope tied around his neck, releasing the net of armor, which plunges into the mountain stream hundreds of feet below. At once this totally spent and contrite man bursts into a gush of tears. At last he has been forgiven. He has been cut free from the awful burden of guilt he has carried for so long, and he can't help but cry uncontrollably. The rest of the story tells how this man gives himself in mission work among the same Indians he once exploited and mistreated.

Our experience of forgiveness in salvation may not be as dramatic, but it is no less real. The question is: For what purpose have we been saved? Was it for us alone? Or was it so we can be light showing others the way and so we can personify (the theological term is *incarnate*) God's love in ministry to others? If a mean, greedy soldier can find his way to mission service through forgiveness, so can we.

Make Your Life Your Argument

In the previous chapter I mentioned the relevance of James 2:14–17 for the idea of getting involved in hands-on mission work. Let me return to that passage again with a more in-depth examination of it. When James writes, "faith without works is dead," he is confronting those who claim to believe but whose lives provide scant evidence of their belief. Actually, he is more direct in his indictment of faith without action when he suggests that ministry to the everyday needs of others is the only adequate proof of belief.

I wonder how many churches are taking this admonition seriously. Either they simply have not given it enough priority, or they lack the backbone to apply James's proof of belief to their members. I heard of one church that does enforce the "faith without works is dead" standard of Christian living. The church challenges every person who joins to find and become involved in some ministry, either within the organization of the church or out in the community. When members do not demonstrate a willingness to serve, the church confronts them with that failure and lets them know that they will need to take up their own towel if they intend to remain members.

Let me ask you something: "What do you believe in? What are you willing to fight for? sacrifice for? die for?" Suppose I came at it another way. Suppose I asked you: "How do you spend your time and money?" Then, based on your answers, I told you: "These are the things you believe in"? Do you see what I mean? For most of us there is a disconnect between what we say we believe and how we behave. When it comes to missions, we say we believe, but we are content to let others do the work. I once heard someone suggest that too many church folk are like the county road crew when it comes to mission work—one person digs, one person patches, another one sweeps, a different one flags, still another supervises, seven watch, and the rest of us pay. James says it is time we took our turn at the shovel. It's time we stopped letting our checkbook do our mission work for us. It's time we signed up, stood up, rolled up our sleeves, and caught up with those who are practicing what James said all believers are to do.

Albert Schweitzer is an excellent example of this conviction. In the 1950s author Norman Cousins paid Schweitzer a visit in Africa, where the doctor, a gifted musician and theologian, ministered for most of his adult life. At the end of his visit, Cousins asked Dr. Schweitzer if he was glad he came to Africa. The jungle doctor said he'd had forty years to think about that question, so there was no hesitation in his reply: Yes, he was very glad. He went on to say:

> As a young man, my main ambition was to be a good minister. I completed my studies; then, after a while I started to teach. I became the principal of the seminary. All this while I had been studying and thinking about the life of Jesus…The more I studied and thought, the more convinced I became that Christian theology had become overcomplicated. In the early centuries after Christ, the beautiful simplicities relating to Jesus became somewhat obscured by conflicting interpretations and incredibly involved dogma growing out of theological debates.
>
> I developed some of my own ideas. Now, what was I to do? Was I to teach…[what] I had been taught but now did not believe? Was I to teach what I believed but [was at variance with those who taught me]?

Faced with these two questions, I decided to do neither. I decided that I would leave the seminary. Instead of trying to get acceptance for my ideas,...I decided I would make my life my argument. I would advocate the things I believed in terms of the life I lived and what I did. Instead of vocalizing my belief in the existence of God within each of us, I would attempt to have my life and work say what I believed.[7]

That's precisely what James says: Make your life your argument. Let your faith express itself in ministry to others. This is what Operation Inasmuch is about—ordinary Christians practicing their faith, making their case for the grace of God with their hands and backs in the dirt and discouragement of their own communities.

7

Mobilizing Volunteers

Everyone can be great because anyone can serve. You don't have to have a college degree to serve. You don't even have to make your subject and your verb agree to serve... You only need a heart full of grace. A soul generated by love.

MARTIN LUTHER KING JR.

One is not born into the world to do everything but to do something.

HENRY DAVID THOREAU

Streshin, a typical *shtetl* or Jewish village in Belarus, supported at least fifteen charitable organizations. There was a Khevre Kedisha, or burial society. The Shomrim society would provide guards to stay with the body from death to burial. The Khevre T'Hilim society came together to read psalms and raise money for charitable projects. The G'miles Khesed Society made interest-free loans to those in need. The women's Lekhem Evyeynim Society collected extra *challah* bread on Thursday

89

mornings and distributed it to needy Jews in time for the Sabbath. The Bikur Kholim society would raise money for families to travel to the city for medical care. They would also harvest ice from the Dnieper every winter and store it in an underground cellar; the rest of the year they delivered ice to those suffering from fever. A Jewish book society raised money for the lending library and invited lecturers from nearby cities. At its height in the 1880s, Streshin's Jewish population numbered 552.[1]

Not many communities can boast of this level of volunteer involvement. Few Christian congregations, who usually enjoy close-knit relationships and unique motivations to serve others, can claim to have so many of their members involved in hands-on ministry as the tiny community of Streshin. In fact, most congregations struggle to enlist the volunteers necessary to staff their ongoing ministries. The idea of mobilizing somewhere between 50 and 100 percent of their average attendance for a new ministry may have some congregational leaders wondering how it can be done. Anticipating this question, in this chapter I want to address some of the issues involved in mobilizing volunteers for Operation Inasmuch. After giving generalized data concerning volunteerism in America and in churches, I will look at the most common, nonbiblical motives people have for getting involved in helping ministries. Understanding why people give themselves to help others will help congregational leaders in their attempt to conduct a successful Operation Inasmuch.

Trends

According to studies conducted by Independent Sector, as many as 110 million Americans volunteer their time and/or talent in all types of services each year. That's an 18 percent increase over the number of volunteers as recently as 1995. "The percentage of adult population volunteering increased by almost 6 percentage points [of the total population]—a significant increase since 1995 when 49% reported volunteering."[2] It would appear that recent emphases on volunteerism are paying off.

On the church front, the numbers are not as good. George Barna reports that only 21 percent of adults volunteer some of their time to help a church in a typical week.[3] So congregations are performing much more poorly than other organizations at recruiting and mobilizing volunteers. I admit that this statistic surprised me, but then I reflected on what I see in the churches I have served. Only about half of the total membership attends with any regularity (not counting Christmas and Easter when the culture demands it). A minority of that number, perhaps half of the regular attenders, ever donate their time in service to the church or ministries of the church. That brings us down to about one-quarter of the total membership volunteering—not far from Barna's number.

A closer look at volunteering in the church is even more revealing. A 1993 Independent Sector survey found that 57 percent of the total volunteer time in congregations was devoted to religious worship and education. Only 8 percent of the volunteer time was allotted to "human services and welfare," which I take to mean benevolent or helping ministries.[4] Surely, we cannot question that we have room for much growth when it comes to involving believers in hands-on ministries. This might also explain in part why some congregational leaders have pounced on Operation Inasmuch as a means of mobilizing their congregants in meaningful ministry. Given the low level of involvement in many congregations, Operation Inasmuch offers great hope for improvement. It is no wonder that congregational leaders, without exception, are hailing Operation Inasmuch as hugely successful when we compare the statistics above to those reported in earlier chapters about the high percentage of people who are participating in Operation Inasmuch.

Before leaving this brief examination of the statistics of volunteerism and the church, I want to share another finding of Independent Sector: "There is continuing interest in encouraging congregations to take a more active role in other federal programs. Congress is currently considering several bills enabling faith-based organizations to compete for other federal program contracts, including those in public health, drug and violence prevention, housing and literacy."[5] Since the release of these findings, President George W. Bush has put the matter on the front burner with his call for more faith-based initiatives nationwide. This can only result in an even greater need for volunteers to staff what will surely be many new programs and initiatives aimed at caring for the hurting and disadvantaged. One view of these developments—the fresh look at faith-based approaches to caring for people and the emergence of initiatives such as Operation Inasmuch—is that need and provision are coming together at just the right time. Perhaps the *kairos* timing mentioned in chapter 1 is more significant than first thought.

Faith and Works

Don't be fooled by the title of this section. It is not another episode in the faith-works debate as they relate to salvation. It is rather a discussion of the relationship between a believer's faith and his or her ministry or service as a ministry volunteer. Chapters 5 and 6 give the biblical rationale for hands-on ministry. For those who are moved by the authority of Scripture the two previous chapters provide sufficient motive for volunteering for an Operation Inasmuch or for any other ministry. It is my contention that congregational leaders should not neglect the biblical models such as Samuel and Isaiah or the directives of Jesus in calling their people to respond to the needs of hurting folk in their community. However, I am realistic enough to know that other motives are often at work when a person says "Yes" to the call to get involved in an Operation Inasmuch. It is wise to examine those other motives when thinking of ways to mobilize believers to get outside the walls of their church buildings to do ministry.

In his comprehensive analysis of caring, Robert Wuthnow found that there is a definite connection between faith and works, or religious convictions and caring.[6] For example, people who have a defined understanding of God's love for them are more likely to be involved in caring activities. The survey that served as the basis for many of Wuthnow's findings indicated that the deeper one's faith is the more likely he or she is to volunteer in a caring capacity. This fact is illustrated by the comment of one Christian woman whose story Wuthnow relates: "The Christian teaching is that we do care for ourselves. God made us, and we're important. But we just need to realize that it's easy to think of ourselves as better than or more important than others. So we need to see others as equal to ourselves and care for them just as much."[7]

Unfortunately, many Christians have not yet recognized the connection between their faith and the kind of works James refers to in the New Testament book that bears his name. They are not unlike what one minister in an urban church saw as he looked out over his congregation one Sunday. He wrote:

> There they sit, row after row of immensely gifted grown-ups, dressed in proper Sunday morning attire, waiting. Waiting for the minister to say the words that will ignite them. Hoping that this Sunday they will be challenged with more than a capital funds campaign for a new family center…there they all sit, people with the nature and gifts of the Divine, fully equipped with every ability necessary to tackle the complex problems of the world. Domesticated by their culture, they long to possess the courage to throw off the obligations of consumerism and spend themselves for the One who has called them.[8]

How does a congregational leader motivate people like this? How does he tap into their desire to make a difference? How does he help them see the benefits of hands-on ministry? He can cite the biblical models and say, "Go and do likewise." He can admonish them according to biblical instructions. But chances are they have heard these before. Then he can season his appeals with a good dose of pragmatism. Without abandoning the theological rationale for caring for others, he can appeal to those motives that have a proven record of moving people from a sedentary faith to an active one. Therefore, we will now turn our attention to those motives.

Incentives for Hands-on Ministry

The literature about volunteerism, including that of the Christian community, has identified several incentives for persons' involvement in hands-on ministry beyond the more spiritual or scriptural ones discussed in earlier chapters. (As long ago as 1991, there were seven hundred articles and books on giving and volunteering, and that number may well have doubled since then.)[9] Independent Sector has become a primary source of information concerning all aspects of volunteerism. Their studies do not always focus on religious groups, churches, and so forth, but their findings help us understand the volunteer mindset. One of their studies revealed the following as the most important reasons people volunteer to help with social service activities:

- feeling compassion for those in need (86%)
- having an interest in the activity or work (72%)
- gaining a new perspective on things (70%)
- the importance of the activity to people the volunteer respects (63%)[10]

The first and fourth reasons in this list lend themselves to recruitment of volunteers for Operation Inasmuch. Compassion for hurting people is completely consistent with the biblical witness, and the influence of congregational leaders, both clergy and laity, make them useful tools in motivating volunteers in the church.

The challenge. Sometimes people just need to be challenged to get involved. One of the best examples of the effectiveness of challenging people is the story of the Peace Corps. On October 14, 1960, after a long day of campaigning for the presidency, John F. Kennedy arrived at the University of Michigan in Ann Arbor at 2:00 a.m. He planned to get some sleep. The press traveling with his entourage had already retired for the evening. But ten thousand University of Michigan students were waiting to hear him speak. They heard him issue a challenge: How many of them, he asked, would be willing to serve their country and the cause of peace by living and working in the developing world? The response was enthusiastic, and the Peace Corps was born. When he became President, John F. Kennedy established the Peace Corps and reissued his challenge to the entire nation. Since 1961, 161,000 Americans have served in 134 nations of the world, demonstrating neighborliness on this tiny, spinning piece of clay we call Earth—all because a group of students were challenged.[11]

We should never underestimate the power of "The Ask," as it has been called. Independent Sector found that *90 percent* of individuals volunteered when asked.[12] I have seen it again and again in congregations. Many people are willing, but they are uncomfortable taking initiative. However, once presented with a genuine opportunity and appropriately challenged, they will respond. I have seen it with Operation Inasmuch. Consider the story of Mary Poole of Clinton, North Carolina.

> I very seldom volunteer. If you ask me, sure, I'll do anything; but I kept waiting for someone to volunteer [to lead Operation Inasmuch]. It kept being in the bulletin, and they would mention it in the announcements on Sunday morning. I thought, "Surely, someone is going to take this [responsibility] because it did so well last year." I would think every Sunday morning that someone was going to take it. It grew heavier and heavier on me. So, finally that one Sunday morning I thought if somebody doesn't take it today, I'll just tell [the pastor] that I will take it and do with it what I can. I don't like to undertake large things like this because I'd rather be a follower. I went up to the pastor after church and asked if anyone had volunteered to lead Operation Inasmuch. He said, "No" I asked if he'd

like for me to try and he said, "Sure." That's how it got started.[13]

Although Mary was not asked specifically to lead Operation Inasmuch, she did respond to the challenge for leadership. My conversations with many other coordinators indicate that church folk anywhere, including some who do not attend regularly, will respond to the challenge to volunteer for Operation Inasmuch.

The desire to make a difference. Many people have a strong desire to make a difference in their community. They want to do something to make their community a better place to live, especially as it relates to human suffering. Robert Wuthnow found that 56 percent of the respondents to his survey concerning why people get involved in caring activities said: "I wanted to do something useful."[14] The famous line by the nineteenth-century reformer Dorothea Dix reflects the same motive for involvement: "In a world where there is so much to do, I felt strongly impressed that there must be something for me to do."[15] A lot of people who have never heard of Dorothea Dix have that same feeling. They live with a desire, the origin of which they are not entirely sure, to do what they can to make a difference.

Gordon Loux and Ronald Wilson further illustrate how widespread this desire is. A man in Massachusetts decided to give a Christmas dinner to anyone in his community who had no place to go. They did not have to be homeless or poor, just alone. As he put it: "My celebration had been so beautiful, but other people were out there sitting in rooms with just a bologna sandwich." He secured the local Elks Hall and wrote a letter to the local paper inviting anyone who was going to be alone on Christmas Day. "The funny thing about it is," he says, "I got thirteen calls the first day. Only three people wanted to come. The other ten wanted to help."[16]

Some of the congregations who have conducted an Operation Inasmuch have had the same experience. One example is First Baptist Church, Lumberton, North Carolina. In their first

Operation Inasmuch, they contacted a local children's home to inquire about some help volunteers from their church might be able to provide on a given Saturday. After discussing the possibilities, administrators at the children's home called back. They wanted the children be on the giving end of helping rather than the receiving, and that is what they did. When congregational leaders are mobilizing volunteers for Operation Inasmuch, they would be wise to tap this huge reservoir of good will, showing how local, hands-on projects can satisfy one's desire to make a difference.

In several cases persons not associated with a congregation got involved because they also wanted to help. On more than one occasion people passing by an Operation Inasmuch home repair project have inquired about what is happening there and have joined in the work. One story has become a kind of folklore at Snyder Memorial. On one roofing project the end of the day was drawing nigh, and the work was far from complete. The volunteers were growing increasingly anxious about their inability to complete their project. Suddenly a man appeared and asked what they were doing. They explained that they were from a church and were attempting to re-roof a lady's home. He asked if he could help and received a quick, "Of course!" When he ascended the ladder, he pulled from a well-worn tool belt a roofing hammer and set about almost single-handedly finishing the job that day. The volunteers were amazed that this man could nail down shingles as fast as they could feed them to him.

When the job was finished, the "Roofing Angel," as he has come to be called, disappeared as suddenly as he had appeared like a cowboy hero quietly riding off into the sunset. Clearly, this unidentified man was not moved to join in the roofing project because of a sermon he heard or because someone persuaded him to help. He joined because of his own desire to help some unskilled but well-intended citizens who were doing what they could to make a difference in their community.

The need to feel good. Anyone who has ever been involved in hands-on ministry has firsthand experience with the "feel good" benefit it brings. Feedback on Operation Inasmuch consistently identifies the fact that doing for others makes us feel good about ourselves. Some examples are: "People were overcome with gratitude and joy that they were able to help others."[17] "Those persons who gave their time and talents gained new acquaintances,...joy in helping someone, and an increased sense of community."[18] "Exhausted, I returned home that afternoon on such a 'high' from what had been accomplished. It was a good feeling to know that my time had been spent helping those less fortunate than I."[19]

Feeling good or a sense of fulfillment is one of the motives Wuthnow discovered in his survey. Eighty-nine percent of the respondents indicated that they received either a great deal of fulfillment or a fair amount of fulfillment in doing things for others.[20] He reports of an advertisement in a Christian magazine by an international relief agency. At the top of the ad was the face of a needy child, dark-skinned, with large, black eyes. In large letters taking about a quarter of the page ad was this line: "It'll Make You Feel Good."[21] Clearly, recruiters for mission volunteers or sponsors of Christian ministries are already making use of the potential of producing fulfilling experiences in promoting their causes. As Robert Wuthnow states in his discussion of the motive of fulfillment, its incentive in caring activities is instant gratification. And everyone knows how well that sells these days.

This may not be as noble as other reasons for volunteering for an Operation Inasmuch project. Many would prefer that it simply be a by-product rather than a motive for doing ministry, but the fact is some people are wondering what is in it for them, whether or not they verbalize that concern. We may be pious in our response to that concern and refuse to appeal to persons' need to feel good, but we will miss the opportunity to help them discover better motives in their well-doing. There is nothing wrong with taking people where they are and nudging them forward in their spiritual growth. It is a fact, as Loux and Wilson say: "When [volunteers] invest themselves in someone else, the gift returns many fold. The selfless act opens a window on the soul. We're not talking about warm fuzzies…We're talking about receiving a gift [through service] that genuinely changes the life of the receiver."[22]

The desire to help neighbors. Despite all the sociological forces that prevent people in the twenty-first century from knowing their neighbors as their grandparents did, there still seems to be a yearning for community. The sense of community has not completely vanished. Indeed, helping neighbors who have needs appeals to a lot of people. Even if the possibility of establishing long-term relationships is remote, the idea of helping one's neighbors is still attractive. As noted in earlier chapters, Operation Inasmuch provides a unique opportunity to satisfy this desire. Recruitment volunteers should exploit it. We have a ready biblical model at our disposal in the good Samaritan by which to legitimize such appeals.

In his research of caring in America, Robert Wuthnow found that the parable of the good Samaritan has enormous influence on people, including those who claim little or no attachment to a Christian congregation. It has become in our culture a model of caring that extends far beyond the Christian community. Wuthnow found that people who knew the story were more likely to be involved in caring activities. Those who have seen it modeled before them by a parent, teacher, or another significant other are even more strongly influenced by it to help victims along the road. His analysis of why this well-known story is so compelling as a motive for caring for others uncovered that its spontaneity and compassion—that the Samaritan stopped in his journey to help one he did not know—are the source of its attraction to so many. In other words, the story attracts people because it does not present a program of caring but a spur-of-the-moment act of compassion.

Mixture of motives. Finally, Wuthnow's analysis of why people get involved in caring for others exposes that they often have more than one reason for doing so. In fact, he found that more often than not, a person's motives are mixed—altruistic and utilitarian. They want to help others, but often some self-interest is involved as well. He cites the comments of one volunteer: "If I stop to think about it, I help out for all kinds of reasons. Maybe it's because I should; it's a matter of responsibility. But there's usually a maze of other motives: a need for self-esteem, approval, status, power; the desire to feel useful, find intimacy, pay back some debt."[23]

Listening to congregational leaders and individual volunteers leads me to the conclusion that church volunteers' motives are mixed as well. As much as we preachers might like to think we are motivating our people to get involved in caring for others with our stem-winding sermons, the truth is other motives are at work as well. Believers are as likely to be moved by their desire to make a difference or the need to feel fulfilled in what they do as by Jesus' "Inasmuch" statement in Matthew 25:40. The parable of the good Samaritan may get their attention and even stimulate their willingness to help a stranger in need. Still, they are seldom unaware of their own need to feel good about themselves and the potential of doing for others as one of the best ways of satisfying that felt need. Mother Teresa may say with all the support of a lifetime of unselfish caring, "Tell them we do it for Jesus,"[24] but the average believer is not so sure.

I reiterate something I have said earlier in this chapter. Congregational leaders have a responsibility to hold forth biblical reasons for ministry, but it is the better part of wisdom to be aware of other reasons people have for getting involved in hands-on projects. If for no other reason, we should remember that behavior has a way of influencing attitudes. Sometimes we do something for one reason, but once we have done it, our motive is influenced by our experience. In recruiting them for Operation Inasmuch, congregational leaders can appeal to their fellow believers' desire for fulfillment or to make a difference with some confidence that the act of caring will validate and cause to come alive some of the traditional biblical teaching about such things.

How to keep them. Mobilizing volunteers involves more than recruitment; it involves doing those things that keep them involved and fulfilled in their work. Plenty of literature on volunteer management is available, though most of it is of a secular nature. Church groups are just beginning to realize the importance of these issues. Marlene Wilson spent fifteen years in secular volunteer management. She developed considerable expertise in identifying the causes of burnout and resignation by volunteers. Recently, she came to the realization that her discoveries in the secular world might also apply to church volunteers. When she investigated that matter, she found that church volunteers experience the same frustrations as those of other organizations. She pressed for more data, and here is what she found. Church volunteers repeatedly say they want and need

- to be carefully interviewed and appropriately assigned to a meaningful task
- to receive training and supervision to enable them to do that task well
- to be involved in planning and evaluating the program in which they participate
- to receive recognition in a way that is meaningful to them
- to be regarded as persons of uniqueness
- to be accepted as valued members of the team[25]

These concerns speak for themselves. I have shared Wilson's findings, not to complicate further the task of the leader of volunteers, but to enhance the quality of that work. Any conscientious leader will want to evaluate how well he or she is doing with the volunteers. Because of the magnitude of an Operation Inasmuch—hundreds of volunteers working a multitude of projects—it may not be easy to address each of them in every experience of Operation Inasmuch, but it would be a mistake to ignore them altogether. As we mobilize believing volunteers to get outside the walls of the church, let us do what we can to keep them mobilized.

Plan the Work, Work the Plan

Great opportunities to help others seldom come, but small ones surround us every day.

SALLY KOCH

Service to others is the rent you pay for your room here on Earth.

MUHAMMAD ALI

The call came about the time I began a one-month sabbatical to write this book. Unlike the one I described from Roger Stancil in chapter 1, this call—not the caller but the inquiry—was fairly common, about once every other week. The caller identified herself as a member of a Lutheran congregation in Fayetteville, less than a mile from our church. She was interested in finding out more about Operation Inasmuch. She said she had heard about it and wanted to know how her church could get involved. I considered giving her the standard response to such an inquiry: Have some of your congregational leaders come to the workshop we are offering in conjunction with the upcoming Operation Inasmuch where you can learn all about it. Then it hit me: Why not help this church plan and execute an Operation Inasmuch and include a write-up of that process as a way of helping other congregational leaders learn how to do one themselves? I proposed to the caller to do just that, and we scheduled a time to talk further about this possibility. In our subsequent conversation, I learned that the pastor of the church had already penciled in Operation Inasmuch as a possible event for the church's celebration of their sixty-fifth anniversary. That was sufficient encouragement for us to call a meeting of the social ministry committee, of which Kathy Arle, my caller, is chair.

This chapter will walk the reader through the entire process of planning an Operation Inasmuch through the experience of St. James Lutheran Church. St. James is a sixty-five-year-old ELCA Lutheran congregation of about 700 members with an average worship attendance of approximately 210. The demographics of the congregation mirror those of other mainline congregations in Fayetteville, North Carolina—a healthy blend of retired, middle-aged civilians, and younger military families. They are served by a full-time, seminary-trained minister, a part-time organist/church musician, and one part-time secretary. Prior to this, they had been involved in a number of local mission endeavors, including Operation Christmas Child, hurricane/ flood relief, and making and distributing quilts to migrants and the Homeless Coalition.

Count the Cost

Jesus says: Count the cost of commitment; before you begin, make sure you can see it through (Lk. 14:25–33). Elsewhere he says: "No one who puts his hand to the plow and looks back is fit for the kingdom of God" (Lk. 9:62). The same can be said of a congregation. No congregation should undertake a ministry without a firm commitment to see it through. This is especially true for an Operation Inasmuch. It is a major undertaking that promises matching rewards, but it requires deep commitment and intense efforts to make it work well. Any congregation considering an Operation Inasmuch should take the time to give it careful consideration, taking it through the appropriate channels of decision-making, bringing as many leaders on board as possible. An Operation Inasmuch that has the blessing of the entire congregation has a better chance of success than the one that does not. Once the congregation experiences it, Operation Inasmuch tends to promote itself. As one coordinator said: "We couldn't stop it now if we wanted to."[1]

St. James's social ministry committee met to consider whether to take on an Operation Inasmuch. The church governing body authorized them to make that decision. Other churches may want to take the matter on to the entire congregation as a way of educating the members to the whys and wherefores of Operation Inasmuch. A well-informed congregation tends to be more supportive. The committee viewed a video about Operation Inasmuch produced and distributed by the Baptist State Convention of North Carolina in 1998. They heard excerpts from letters from churches that have conducted an Operation Inasmuch.

On my way into the meeting, I saw a copy of the church's directory. I noticed that the church's mission statement was printed on the front cover: "St. James Lutheran Church, a caring community of Christian believers, affirm our faith in the Gospel by worship, prayer, outreach, Christian education, fellowship and good stewardship. We share our faith and Lutheran heritage with all, showing Christ's love and saving grace." I read this statement to them and pointed out that Operation Inasmuch provides ways to do all the things mentioned in their mission statement—worship, pray, reach out, educate, grow their fellowship, and be good stewards. Chapters 2 and 3 in this book offer ample evidence for my claim.

The committee members asked questions to clarify issues pertaining to the logistics of how it works. We will address these issues in detail in this chapter. Then they decided. By nine to none, with one abstention, they decided to "Go for it!" The lone abstainer said she did not vote because she was "too old," to which her fellow members quickly responded that she was not and that she could certainly do something to help.

Leadership

A word about leadership is appropriate at this point. The senior pastor's support for Operation Inasmuch is critical. As a senior pastor myself, I realize that every new event or program that comes down the pike clamors for his or her support and that the pastor faces limits as to how much he or she can do. But since Operation Inasmuch is designed to mobilize as much of the congregation as possible, the senior pastor's involvement is paramount. That involvement is more than preaching sermons or writing articles in the church newsletter. It's showing up on the appointed day, sporting work clothes, demonstrating a commitment to hands-on ministry. The pastor of St. James was involved in the initial decision concerning Operation Inasmuch. She demonstrated a can-do attitude in the discussions. She was not intimidated by either her or the congregation's lack of experience with anything such as Operation Inasmuch.

The planning and implementation of Operation Inasmuch should be assigned to a committee or ad hoc group of leaders, such as a missions committee, or social ministry committee. One coordinator I interviewed suggested that a special, handpicked task force be put in place to plan and execute Operation Inasmuch.[2] His conviction comes from a concern with infamous church bureaucracies that can unnecessarily stifle the vision for a new ministry. Whether a congregation assigns Operation Inasmuch to a standing committee or selects an ad hoc group to plan and conduct it will be determined by that congregation's structure and history. As a practical matter, this group should be involved in the decision of whether to undertake an Operation Inasmuch. Ownership impacts vision, and vision impacts the group's enthusiasm and perseverance. These leaders should be self-starters, dependable, not easily discouraged, and have a vision for the possibilities of Operation Inasmuch.

One person, either a staff person or a lay leader, usually the chair of the assigned committee or group, is to function as the coordinator. This person must be granted appropriate authority for carrying out this vital role, such as assigning volunteers to projects or making "executive decisions" concerning supplies, etc. Some congregations have found it useful to set up a temporary office in the church facilities for the coordinator as a base of operations. As with anything else that happens in the church, the competence and commitment of the congregational leaders supporting and coordinating an Operation Inasmuch will go a long way in determining its success. It is wise to designate an "understudy" or apprentice coordinator to work alongside the coordinator throughout the first Operation Inasmuch. Anticipating that the church will want to conduct the ministry again, it is best to train leadership for future events. Coordinating an Operation Inasmuch is a demanding responsibility for several months. Most laypersons who undertake this responsibility are eager to share it, then pass it off to a fresh leader the next time around.

Where possible it is desirable, but not absolutely necessary, to apprentice an Operation Inasmuch with another congregation that has some experience with it. Most experienced congregations are happy to share their experiences with others and to work volunteers from other churches into their projects to help them learn the process. Surely this is a sensible approach, but it will be difficult in that most congregations that have experience with Operation Inasmuch as of the release of this book are in the southeastern United States. Congregations located in other parts of the country or world will have to rely on their own ingenuity and the adequacy of these instructions. Many of the coordinators I interviewed suggested that the best way to get started with Operation Inasmuch is to start small, perhaps with two or three projects, then expand as experience and confidence grows.

In reflecting on my first meeting with St. James's social ministry committee, I must admit that my presentation of Operation Inasmuch was designed to appeal to the desire of the committee to see their church do something significant, something that would bring meaning and fulfillment to those who participated, and something that would unite them in what has become a defining community event. I did not appeal to their sense of obedience to the biblical imperatives to minister to human hurts and hopes. Other than references to Matthew 25:40, I did not mention any of the biblical passages explored in this book, nor did anyone else. If I had been preaching about Operation Inasmuch, no doubt my message would have been heavily laced with biblical references. This confession reveals something important about motives for doing an Operation Inasmuch. Rather than grounding our decision to do it in what Jesus says about doing for others, we naturally move to those motives that are most self-serving—having an experience that will mean much to us as individual believers, seeing our church do something noteworthy in the community, and perhaps getting some positive PR as a side benefit.

This is symptomatic of the way congregations usually make decisions. As mentioned in the preceding chapter, Robert Wuthnow found that persons seldom have only one reason for getting involved in hands-on ministries. If this is the way it is for individual believers, is it not also true for congregations? For now, let us recognize that my failure to connect the "What?" of Operation Inasmuch with its "Why?" can serve as a warning to other congregational leaders to avoid the same mistake.

Selecting a Date

One of the first decisions is to select a date on which Operation Inasmuch will take place. Naturally, the date should not conflict with any other church activity and should avoid, as much as possible, major conflicts in the community. (Snyder Memorial is located in the heart of basketball country, not far from "Tobacco Road." Therefore, we always check the dates of the Atlantic Coast Conference basketball tournament in March before we establish the March Operation Inasmuch.) Another consideration when selecting a date is that it should allow sufficient lead time for planning. The first time a church does an Operation Inasmuch requires up to six months lead time from initial decision to the actual date as indicated in the time line below. The time line can be compressed down to three to four months if the planning group is willing to meet more frequently. In succeeding years, less time will be needed, as a congregation's experience base expands. The St. James committee agreed to schedule their Operation Inasmuch to coincide with those of about two dozen other churches in Fayetteville. They wanted to experience the camaraderie of working alongside volunteers from other churches where possible. This significantly reduced the time available to plan their Operation Inasmuch, but it proved to be the right decision.

Operation Inasmuch Time Line	
-SIXTEEN WEEKS	**Adopt Operation Inasmuch**
	Assign planning/organization to a ministry team
-FOURTEEN WEEKS	**Select Operation Inasmuch Coordinator**
	Select date
	Identify cooperating agencies
-TWELVE WEEKS	**Brainstorm possible projects**
	Evaluate ideas according to established criteria
-TEN WEEKS	**Develop strategy for communications**
	Recruit project team leaders
	Continue evaluating projects
	Create awareness in congregation
-SIX WEEKS	**Launch sign-up process**
	Continue evaluating projects
-TWO WEEKS	**Polish details on projects**
	Arrange for materials for all projects
	Order food for lunches
	Press release (if desired)
	Arrange for photography
-ONE WEEK	**Complete sign-up process**
	Assign all volunteers to projects
	Communicate all details to project team leaders
EVENT WEEK	**OPERATION INASMUCH**
+TWO WEEKS	**Evaluate experience**

Identifying Projects

After reaching a decision to go forward with an Operation Inasmuch, the St. James committee moved immediately into a brainstorming session about possible projects. The identification of projects and project leaders is one of the first tasks in the planning phase of Operation Inasmuch. Once I shared with the committee a few of the projects other churches had undertaken, they were able to name several others according to their experiences in local missions. These included yard work for homebound persons, a sewing project utilizing their existing quilting group, construction of wheelchair ramps for disabled persons, repair of substandard homes qualified by a local agency, paint-up/fix-up at the City Rescue Home, a baby shower for expectant mothers in a local maternity home, and so on. The atmosphere in the room was electric. The more the committee talked, the more energized they became, dreaming of how many of their congregation could be mobilized in one day to minister to so many persons at their points of need.

A frequently asked question is: How do you come up with projects, especially for all age groups? A good place to begin is mission projects already undertaken by the congregation, perhaps at various times in the year. These projects usually bring with them experienced and willing leaders. The planning group should be creative in brainstorming ideas for projects. To assist in a congregation's initial experience with Operation Inasmuch, a list of projects actually done by congregations is provided in appendix A. Even more important than the quantity of projects is the quality of the projects, determined by their "missions quotient." Over the years, we have developed criteria by which we evaluate the value of project ideas and their missions quotient:

- Can it be completed in one day?
- Do we have people who are willing and able to do the work?
- Does it appeal to a sufficient number of people or a particular age group?
- Does it respond to human hurts and hopes or offer a way to share the gospel?

- Do we have an adequate number of jobs for churchwide participation?
- Can we obtain sufficient resources to complete it?

A major component of identifying possible projects depends on which organizations in the community are open to partnering with churches on projects such as Operation Inasmuch. Most communities have nonprofit service organizations or government agencies that are knowledgeable of the needs of persons and families in the community. Usually they are willing to share that information, provided appropriate assurances are given as to confidentiality and intentions. Some nonprofits willing to partner with congregations are hospices, Habitat for Humanity, the local benevolent organization (each one has a unique name), and the Salvation Army. Some government agencies often willing to provide useful information about the community are the Department of Social Services, the Council on Older Adults, and schools. Partnering with established organizations is a win-win proposition. As I have described in earlier chapters, most churches have experienced a windfall in public relations as well as in effectiveness when they have been able to collaborate with such groups.

The St. James committee made an important decision near the end of their initial meeting. They recognized the importance of informing their congregation about this new undertaking. The pastor suggested that someone could share with the congregation in the upcoming Sunday services. Two laypersons in the group agreed to do this. Normally, the pastor shares important announcements, but this time laypersons did it. This pattern was followed throughout the public communications. That is symbolic of the fact that Operation Inasmuch is lay-driven. This is one of the benefits identified back in chapter 2—it gives prominence to laypersons. St. James was wise to establish that priority from the outset.

Shaping the Vision

In their second meeting, the St. James's social ministry committee refined their list of projects for Operation Inasmuch.

The committee chair had summarized the brainstorming from the first meeting. They applied the criteria given earlier to the list to ensure that each project had adequate missions quotient and potential for Operation Inasmuch.

Their project list consisted of thirteen separate projects, including home repair, construction of a wheelchair ramp, lunch preparation and delivery, sewing quilts to be given to homeless persons, sewing walker bags to be given to nursing home patients, painting the exterior of the home of an elderly couple, yard work, and many others. They reviewed the list to ensure that all ages of participants would be provided for. They estimated the number of volunteers required for each project and measured the grand total to see whether they were adequately challenging the entire congregation.

Project Leaders

The next step was to identify project leaders. These persons are critical for a successful Operation Inasmuch. Each one must have the skills necessary to complete the project. Also, he or she should be dependable. If an insufficient number of persons choose to be involved in his or her project, he or she should be able to see it through. Completing this step in the process of planning an Operation Inasmuch usually gives the group responsible for this planning a clear picture of their probable success. You may hear audible sighs of relief in the group when a qualified leader is identified for each project. At this point the planning group will begin to feel confident that their congregation can actually pull this off.

Communicating the Opportunity

The committee then turned their attention to creating awareness in their congregation about the opportunities and challenges of Operation Inasmuch. The most effective approach to publicity is to strategize for it, to develop a plan that is progressive and creative. Since the goal of Operation Inasmuch is to mobilize as much of the congregation as possible for one day, it is necessary to do whatever it takes to get their attention and help them want to be involved. That requires more than a blurb in the church's newsletter. St. James did, indeed, develop a comprehensive strategy of publicity and motivation:

- Verbal announcements in worship services—five weeks out from Operation Inasmuch
- Bulletin inserts—four weeks out
- Teens to make and display posters—three weeks out
- Telephone entire membership asking them to pray and sign up—three weeks out
- Sunday school teachers to announce the date and projects in classes—two weeks out

Some congregations have become quite creative with publicity and motivation. One church enlarged a picture of people (not professionals) working on the exterior of a house to the size of about five feet square and cut it into numerous puzzle pieces. They asked their members to sign up by signing one of the puzzle pieces. When a piece had about five signatures, it was put in place on a large sheet displayed in a prominent place. As the congregation staffed all the projects, they completed the puzzle picture of one of those projects.[3]

Another church put up sawhorses in the large gathering space of their facility. A sign describing one of their Operation Inasmuch projects was attached to each sawhorse along with a board containing a list of volunteers for that project. Each project had a sawhorse, creating high visibility for Operation Inasmuch. They left the sawhorses up for several weeks, creating a great deal of interest and involvement. I was not surprised to learn that this church had 75 percent of their average attendance participating.[4]

Yet another church dedicates a Sunday to signing up for their Operation Inasmuch. Prior to that day, the entire congregation receives by mail a list and description of all the projects and a reminder of the sign-up day. The pastor preaches on some aspect of hands-on missions or reaching out to the community. Following the worship service, the congregation is dismissed to the front lawn, where tables are set up with information about each of the projects and project leaders to answer inquiries. Sign-up sheets allow volunteers to indicate their desire to be involved in Operation Inasmuch. The immediacy of this approach has contributed to the continued mobilization of a significant portion of this congregation.[5]

Fine Tuning

As the St. James social ministries committee continued to meet, two things happened. First, they refined their plans and recruited volunteers. Second, excitement and confidence built as they began to see how they could meet this challenge. Kathy Arle provided superb leadership—distributing a summary of developments since their last meeting for everyone, updating the committee on all fronts, and guiding them through a thorough discussion of all the details of the planning process. She demonstrated well the primary gift required for the coordinator—organization. Since the planning of an Operation Inasmuch is saturated with details, the coordinator must have the ability to manage details well. His or her primary leadership group will be able to function better when their chair is "on top of things."

Refining projects and recruitment of volunteers. At the beginning of the third and fourth meetings of the social ministry committee, Arle distributed a complete list of all projects, including their team leaders and a description of what each project involved. Because the committee had done a good job of educating the congregation about Operation Inasmuch, people responded well to the opportunity to be team leaders. Only a couple of the projects did not have team leaders by the committee's third meeting, and they quickly identified capable persons to fill those positions. Members of the church also responded well to initial opportunities to volunteer to work in Operation Inasmuch. Their projects were about half-staffed after the first sign-up period. By their fourth meeting—after most of their publicity strategy had been implemented—more than one hundred volunteers had signed up, with almost all the projects fully staffed. With almost two weeks remaining in the sign-up period, they had reached the 50 percent level of participation for their congregation, with the real possibility of reaching 60 or 65 percent. Is it any wonder that excitement and confidence grew with each meeting?

A question that often surfaces in the planning of an Operation Inasmuch until a congregation gains some experience with it is: What do we do if we have too many volunteers? This is an important question and should be dealt with as soon as possible. One answer is to assign more volunteers to those projects that can accommodate more people. This may mean that the project will be completed in less time, but this is preferred to under-utilization of volunteers. A better way to address this issue is to plan additional projects to utilize all the volunteers who sign up. Each volunteer should be valued, and the best way to do that is give him or her worthwhile tasks for the day. Nothing will hinder future recruitment as much as under-utilization of volunteers. A wise planning group will "hold back" a project or two until they see how many volunteers they have. That is, the planning group will do the background work on the projects without promoting them in the publicity about Operation Inasmuch. If more persons than expected volunteer, these projects can be worked into the plan fairly easily. To make use of all persons who wanted to be involved, St. James added a couple of projects in the last couple of weeks prior to Operation Inasmuch.

Other details the St. James social ministry committee addressed in these follow-up meetings included what the sack lunches for the volunteers should include, how many lunches to prepare, supplies needed to complete some of the projects, the process to follow for reimbursement of expenses incurred in purchasing those supplies, and prayer support for the endeavor. None of these issues are difficult, but they do require adequate discussion for the effort to be well organized. It is best that these matters be worked out in committee, as opposed to the coordinator or some other individual making "executive decisions." I noted that the person leading the prayer effort was the one committee member who abstained in the initial decision to undertake an Operation Inasmuch. Not only had she become involved, but she had developed a rather creative way to get many of the congregation involved in praying for all aspects of Operation Inasmuch, especially for good weather.

At some point in the planning process, the planning group must address the liability issue. Unfortunately, we live in a time when anyone can be sued for just about any reason. Churches are not exempt from liability even in the normal course of conducting their regular ministries. Since most churches have insurance policies in place covering their liabilities, usually it is sufficient to communicate with the local insurance agent about what the church is planning for Operation Inasmuch and ensuring that these activities are, in fact, covered by the church's policy. Usually, you should communicate in writing so the church will have an adequate record should any liability issues arise later. While this is not a major concern, it should not be overlooked. I have never learned of a congregation that was discouraged from sending volunteers out due to liability concerns expressed by an insurance carrier.

Communications. The committee reviewed their publicity strategy each time they met. They had devised a thorough plan, and it worked well. Responses from the congregation evinced that. Most of the committee members reported enthusiastic responses from individuals in the congregation as they spoke to them about Operation Inasmuch. Some of them had already signed up. Others could not participate due to health concerns or personal conflicts, but were supportive nonetheless. The committee members were clearly buoyed by the feedback they received from the congregation.

They agreed early on to telephone every family in the congregation about two weeks prior to Operation Inasmuch—something that is easier to do for a smaller congregation than a larger one. They developed a guide to be used in this telephoning.

The guide is presented in appendix D. Clearly, this aspect of their communications proved most effective. One committee member reported that in her conversations with members of the church, she said: "We've done the work for you; all we're asking is that you show up, and we'll tell you what to do." Any church willing to undertake this task as part of their communication with their members will experience stronger support both spiritually and in terms of the number of volunteers who participate.

Commissioning Service and Celebration

Once the committee had a handle on the planning of their Operation Inasmuch and their confidence in executing those plans had developed sufficiently, they were ready to consider two other important aspects of a successful Operation Inasmuch. I suggested that they hold a brief commissioning service in which they gather at their church early on the Saturday of Operation Inasmuch and worship together. The purpose of this gathering is to remember why they are doing Operation Inasmuch and the priority of relating to those persons they will be serving during the day. The pastor would lead them in this worship, perhaps speaking from Matthew 25:40, clarifying biblical motives for their undertaking, connecting the "Why?" with the "What?" of Operation Inasmuch. The group agreed that such a service would add value to the entire experience, and the pastor eagerly accepted the responsibility for planning and leading it.

I also suggested that it would be good for the congregation to celebrate their mission service. This is usually done in the regular Sunday worship services the day following an Operation Inasmuch. One church celebrates at a barbecue event at the end of the day on the Saturday of Operation Inasmuch, but most churches find it difficult to reassemble volunteers once they have disbursed from their projects. At Snyder, we devoted whole worship experiences to this celebration on a couple of occasions. I have learned that others have as well with similar positive results.

Such a celebration brings at least two benefits. One, everyone learns of the experiences of fellow members when those are shared with the entire congregation. Two, the congregation gains a more accurate perspective of the impact they have made on their community when reports are shared in a larger group. Most congregations that include such a celebration in their experience of Operation Inasmuch report that it was one of the most moving times of worship in recent years. One coordinator says:

> During the celebration service the day after the project, a nurse who did blood pressure checks at a grocery store said she had been a nurse for many years and taking blood pressure was routine for her. She said she never looked at her job as a ministry until Operation Inasmuch. Now she would look at her job differently. Others told of how they tried to find excuses not to participate. However, they came and were blessed beyond words.[6]

Organizing Lunch

Providing lunch for all volunteers allows them to stay on the job and creates at least one more project in which to involve people who do not feel they have a skill to be used elsewhere. The menu should be simple, usually sandwiches, chips, a piece of fruit, and/or cookies. The number of lunches to be prepared should correspond roughly to the total number of volunteers, plus about twenty percent more. It is a good idea to include the residents of any home that is being repaired and of any residence where a wheelchair ramp is constructed.

Project team leaders report to "Command Central" the number of lunches needed for each project. That number is added to the report of other team leaders, and the grand total is reported to the "Lunch Preparation/Delivery Team." Names, addresses, and directions to each off-site project should be available for those making deliveries. Delivery should be completed before noon. Of course, volunteers working in projects conducted at the church eat lunch there.

Home Stretch

As with any major congregational event, no amount of advance planning completely eliminates the intensity of the last few days leading up to the actual day of the event. Some details simply should not be done too early. Of course, these are commonsense items of good organization. However, to facilitate the planning and execution of your first Operation Inasmuch, most of these details are provided here.

Final details. Ten days to one week prior to Operation Inasmuch, the coordinator reconfirms with each project team leader his or her preparations for the project and assists in clarifying any final details. This may include room arrangements in the church for the project, reservations for church vehicles to be used in the project, or any special needs required by the project, such as sufficient extension cords for a sewing project. Appendices E and F, in their "Sample Operation Inasmuch Letters to Project Leaders," list instructions to project leaders that St. James used. They sent one letter about two weeks prior to the event, and the other the week of the event. These are excellent models of good communication and organization. At this same point the coordinator reconfirms with the pastor or appropriate leader the plans for the commissioning service to begin Operation Inasmuch.

About one week prior to Operation Inasmuch, each project team leader should receive a complete list of volunteers for that individual project. The list should include phone numbers. The project leader should use this list to contact each volunteer several days before Operation Inasmuch. The purpose of this contact is threefold: to confirm the person's commitment to serve on that project, to give last-minute instructions as to any supplies or tools that may be required for the project, and to give directions to the project if it is located away from the church. The planning group should have devised a way to notify each volunteer of their placement on the particular project. This may be as simple as posting lists on bulletin boards and printing them in church newsletters and worship bulletins. Two or three weeks before the event, a telephone committee may attempt to contact each volunteer to communicate the placements. Even with such communication plans, and although volunteers will have signed up for a particular project, until they hear from their project leader the final week they may not be aware that in fact they have been placed on that project.

Some miscellaneous details to be covered in the last days leading up to Operation Inasmuch are:

- Provide child care at the church for young families—usually only through lunch time (preferably for children five years old and younger).
- Have project team leaders provide their own coolers for ice on the job.
- Arrange for photographs and video to record the day's activities and to be used in future publicity.
- Establish a "Command Central" (usually in the church office) to answer last-minute questions.
- Arrange for cellular phones to be at each project to facilitate communications, and make sure Command Central has the numbers.
- Arrange for trash removal for those projects that require it; this may include making arrangements for a dump truck.
- Obtain all work permits for those projects that require them.
- Prepare a press release of the church's plans, and see that the appropriate media sources receive it.
- Label every piece of equipment and tool possible for recovery at the end of the day.
- Reaffirm with people and organizations you will be serving that they are expecting you to come on the specific date.

If you have done all these things, you have done all the Lord requires of you. You are ready for Operation Inasmuch. Be confident that God will honor your preparations and use your efforts to take his love and grace outside the walls of your church.

9

Mission Outpost

Inasmuch as ye have done it unto one of the least of these my brethren, ye have done it unto me.

JESUS (MT. 25:40, KJV)

In his book *The Gathered and Scattered Church*, Edward Hammett echoes many others at the beginning of the twenty-first century when he says current American culture is more like that in which the first-century church functioned than ever before. Consequently, it has become urgent that the church respond to the changes in its environment by "activating *all* God's people into ministry, dispersing them into a world of darkness as salt, light, and leaven, sending them out as priests in the midst of searching persons."[1] If Hammett is right, and virtually everyone who has written about the church in the last ten years agrees with his assessment, then many are the churches that will use Operation Inasmuch as a means of activating God's people for ministry.

Consider two images of the church, both from the American West. The first is a fort. Its high walls keep its residents safe. Soldiers keep watch on the walls for "hostiles" who might want to break in and plunder the treasures of the fort and the people who live there. The fort is an island of security in the midst of unfriendly territory.

The second image is that of an outpost. It, too, has walls; but its primary purpose is not to keep those inside safe and sound, but to send them out into the frontier to subdue it and make it safe for all. Like the fort, the outpost houses soldiers, but only temporarily. They come to the outpost only to "resupply" themselves and to rest until they are ready to be deployed again to the frontier.

Too many churches today are forts that promote security for insiders and treat outsiders as threats. Hammett and scores of others are trying to help congregations see the need to be outposts while there is still time for a conversion. Operation Inasmuch fits the outpost model of church. It offers a way to deploy believers where they are needed most.

I have made the case in this book that Operation Inasmuch is an effective way of mobilizing believers to get outside the walls of their church buildings to minister to the human hurts and hopes of their local communities. In the previous chapter we saw how one congregation, St. James Lutheran Church, accepted this proposition and planned their first Operation Inasmuch. In this chapter we will evaluate their experience.

Reading the Orders

When I arrived at St. James Church early on the Saturday of Operation Inasmuch, I found a buzz of activity already developing. Members talked about the projects they would be doing and gave thanks for the beautiful weather that day. You could sense the enthusiastic anticipation about the day's work. Members were introducing themselves to one another. Although members of the same congregation, many attend different

Sunday worship services and seldom see each other. More than a few were bringing sewing machines into the church to be used in making walker bags for nursing home patients, food for lunches, and materials to be sorted and assembled in Easter bags for needy children. The church building was slowly being converted into a mission outpost.

Just before eight o'clock, Pastor Louise Hilbert herded all the volunteers into the sanctuary for a brief commissioning service. All ages assembled in the stained-glass, vaulted ceiling worship center. I spotted a young girl, maybe five years old, in pigtails, men in jeans and old sweatshirts, and women in casual clothes. They had come to work, but first they would begin with worship. That is as it should be for followers of Jesus. Everything begins with worship.

The pastor, too, was dressed for the day—jeans and a sweatshirt. The excitement in her voice was evident. Her words came rapidly, and her tone was upbeat. She led the congregation of about seventy-five people (some had already gone to their worksites) in a responsive reading of the Lord's Prayer and the Apostles' Creed. By these time-honored declarations of Christian faith, they remembered who and whose they are. They touched the foundations of their faith like the Notre Dame football team touching the famous header over the passageway that leads from their locker room onto the football field.

The pastor then read the "Inasmuch" passage from Matthew 25. As I sat there listening to those familiar lines and looked around at the Lutherans mobilized and ready to deploy into the community, I could not help but wonder what they were thinking when they heard the "I was" statements of Jesus—"I was sick and you visited me...; I was naked and you clothed me...; I was in prison and you came to me." Did those words mean more in this setting than when they serve as the launching pad for a Sunday morning sermon, when the congregation is dressed in their Sunday finest thinking about which restaurant they will go to when church lets out? Did the fact they were literally on the edge of actually doing what Jesus said in that passage give his words a different meaning?

Pastor Hilbert did not miss the opportunity to make an immediate application of Jesus' sayings to her congregation. She said: "Some of you will help people today by making quilts that will be given to expectant mothers and homeless people. Some of you will do it by working at the block party. Some of you will do it by preparing lunches for all the volunteers. Some of you will do it by building a wheelchair ramp. And some of you will minister to others by sewing walker bags to be given to patients at nursing homes." It was like a commanding officer standing before her troops reading their orders as they are about to move out, but these troops did not carry weapons with them; they carried the Word: "Inasmuch as ye have done it unto one of the least of these my brethren, ye have done it to me."

The pastor's closing prayer was a celebration of ministry and a blessing: "Lord, you have given us many different gifts, and today we have the chance to use them for you. Thank you for these gifts and these opportunities of ministry. Open our eyes and hearts to the needs of the people we meet today. Give us a spirit of cooperation as we work together. Use every part of us in your work. Help us sense your presence in what we do today. Bind us together as brothers and sisters in Christ. Amen." The commissioning service ended with the blessing from the pastor: "Go in peace. Serve the Lord." The congregation responded: "Thanks be to God." Thus these enthusiastic, energetic Lutherans were commissioned to minister in the name of Jesus Christ.

Deployment

The list of projects St. James was able to complete in their Operation Inasmuch is impressive:

- built one wheelchair ramp for an elderly, disabled man
- painted a house for an elderly couple
- cleaned a yard for an eighty-five-year-old, single woman

- made more than one hundred walker bags
- made twenty-five quilts—including five baby quilts—to be given to expectant mothers
- assembled five hundred Easter bags with assorted toys, candies, and a gospel message to be given to children of poverty in two public schools
- held a baby shower for five residents at a maternity home
- checked the blood pressure of about one hundred seventy-five people at three locations
- completed repairs on the exterior of the home of a seventy-six-year-old widow
- collected twenty-five pints of blood in a blood drive
- prepared and delivered about one hundred fifty lunches to volunteers and recipients of ministry

In a single day in Operation Inasmuch, between nine hundred and a thousand people were touched in some way by their ministry, either as recipients of ministry or as volunteers!

Mary Jane Baker is an example of the impact of hands-on ministry in a local community. As an eighty-five-year-old, single woman with no children and little family, but a glowing faith in God, she depends on the compassion of other believers to help her. Because one of the members of St. James Church already had a relationship with Miss Baker, the cleaning of her yard was added to the list of their projects early on in the planning process. She was eager to talk about the help she received through Operation Inasmuch:

> I never had anyone do this kind of thing for me before. Nobody thinks about the old lady. I know one of the ladies who is working here today. She told the folks at St. James that I needed help. They're doing a general cleaning of the yard. It hasn't been done since last August. There are some teenagers working here today. They're doing a fantastic job! I'm proud of it. I feel so good 'bout all this, good in the Lord 'cause he's so good to me. This is one of the ways he's good to me, sending these folks to do this work. He says it's better to give

than receive. That's right. I'm happy 'bout them coming to see 'bout me and do things for me. I'm just happy.[2]

The most significant impact was on the volunteers. Robin Ramirez helped organize the painting project. The elderly couple whose house was painted are her neighbors, the Walls. She explained that the Walls had planned to hire painters until unexpected surgery depleted their funds. When her church began talking about helping people in the community, Robin suggested painting the Walls's home as a project. Her enthusiasm was not simply that she was a bridge between the need of her neighbors and God's people on mission for Him, but that her church was mobilized for ministry. "I've never been part of an attempt by a church to do so many things," Ramirez said, "and I find it amazing. One hundred thirty people is a lot of people. I would expect that for a church dinner, but not for this. I think it's wonderful."[3]

Dave Gorman, volunteer in the wheelchair ramp project, shared others' enthusiasm for the work of Operation Inasmuch. His enthusiasm came not from seeing a neighbor helped, but from meeting the real need of someone he did not know—a man whose legs are severely crippled from arthritis. This man slowly and painfully made his way down and up the steps of his mobile home every day to visit his wife who lives in a nursing home. Moved by the man's circumstances, Gorman had this to say about his church's response to them: "I think the church is really excited about it. This kind of mission work is effective because it goes back to people helping people."[4]

Larry Hilbert was the team leader for the home repair project. He confirmed the assessment of many who have participated in an Operation Inasmuch when he said: "I think one of the things that is good about this program is it's a one-day commitment where you come in and do what you can and then you walk away knowing the job is done."[5]

Others noted the variety in projects offered in Operation Inasmuch: "There are so many options for people. If there are ten different things to choose from, chances are one of those things will suit you and your abilities. This allows more people to contribute."[6]

Mariel Runkle was among those who planned Operation Inasmuch for St. James Church. She watched the process move from anxious decision to completion. Understandably, she was pleased with the results. While taking bags of goodies to be given to children and tying on cards explaining that the bags represent God's love for them, Runkle said: "I think it's fantastic. I really do. I think the participation has been great, and, of course, the cause is great. Everyone has been happy and pleased with what they're doing."[7]

In church life those who are most heavily invested in a ministry are often the ones who gain spiritual insight from that experience. Such was the case for Kathy Arle, coordinator of St. James's Operation Inasmuch. Her life revolved around Operation Inasmuch for several weeks. She gave more of herself in the project than any other person. She, too, watched and guided the process from tentative, even skeptical, commitment to fulfillment on that March Saturday when more of her fellow church members than ever rolled up their sleeves and went to work in hands-on ministry. Consequently, she struggled to keep her emotions under control when she spoke about her feelings about the end result. She was not simply pleased; she was humbled. "This has been the one of the most significant things I've ever done," she said. "It's been one of the most God-led things without a question in my life in a long time. I've had a lot of things in my life when I felt God was working, but this has been near the top of the list."[8]

Pastor Louise Hilbert added: "Operation Inasmuch has exceeded my expectations in the number of people involved and the broad nature of the projects."[9] She viewed the events of the day through a different lens than anyone else. She observed the effect of the work on her flock. Commenting on that very thing, she said: "I have been delighted to see the people who have offered themselves today. Some of these people I don't see in a lot of church activities, and they have been touched in some way to come and be part of this. It has certainly helped to foster a stronger sense of community within our fellowship."[10]

An experienced congregational leader, Pastor Hilbert did not overlook the impact of Operation Inasmuch on her leadership. Commenting on its value for future church projects, she said: "This whole experience will give me as the leader of the church more leverage to challenge the congregation to respond to other needs. It's the right kind of leverage, not manipulation, but built on growth and discipleship."[11]

Volunteers spoke of their motives for being involved as they reflected on their participation. Ryan Johnson, a ten-year-old boy who helped with the wheelchair ramp project, acknowledged that he did not follow his usual Saturday morning routine—sleep late and watch cartoons most of the morning. When asked about his involvement, he said: "It makes me feel good to be doing this kind of work…I'm helping other people. I'm here with members of my family."[12] One teenager on the yard-cleaning project had this to say: "For me, it's the feeling I get afterwards. It's really rewarding, helping people less fortunate. Right now I could be sitting on my couch at home doing nothing, but I'd rather be out here doing this."[13]

Helga Braboy led the walker bag project. She noted the hands-on appeal of Operation Inasmuch. As she threaded her sewing machine, she spoke with pins held in one side of her mouth: "I am willing to do anything, but I want to be useful. That's what makes this kind of thing enjoyable; it's helpful for someone." One of the volunteers who worked with her had another motive for giving a Saturday to make bags to hang on the walkers of nursing home patients. She had once broken her leg and had to use a walker for a time. "I remember what that was like," she said. "I would plan my trips through the house to take things with me. I know from experience the value of these walker bags."[14]

Reflecting on her experience as leader of the baby shower project at a maternity home, Alyson Wood made significant discoveries about herself and her church through Operation Inasmuch. She said:

I've been thinking about something that was said to me before the shower. One of the ladies who donated a good portion of her children's clothing told me that she "hoped they appreciated it." I responded by saying that I was sure they would be very grateful for everything, new and old. What I wish I'd said was: "It doesn't matter whether THEY appreciate it or not. What matters is what we're doing for them." I mulled this over in my head the whole day of the shower and came up with that resolution. I'm glad that the moms were so lovely and grateful, but I don't think my experience with Operation Inasmuch would've changed if they weren't. I got to meet so many people at St. James that I've never known. I got to see so much generosity on the part of our congregation. I got to spend a lot of extra time in prayer over different aspects of the project. This was a good experience for me and I've learned some surprising things about myself and other people.[15]

Reflections and feelings expressed throughout the day of St. James's Operation Inasmuch mirrored those of other churches reported in earlier chapters. They are amazingly predictable. With thorough planning, broad participation, and a clear connection to the biblical basis for mission work, any congregation can expect to see their members energized and humbled by their experience with Operation Inasmuch. A paragraph from "The Messenger," the St. James newsletter, says it well:

We accomplished so much, had great fellowship, had fun, AND served in Jesus' name. Thank you to all who were present Saturday and to all who couldn't be with us Saturday but helped us from your homes. Together, WE DID IT!!![16]

Even before St. James had completed their day of hands-on ministry, I asked their pastor, Louise Hilbert, if she thought they would do it again. Without hesitation, she said: "I think so. I don't think there's any question about it. I've already heard from some of the guys here: 'The next time we do this…'"[17]

Sore Muscles and Smiles

When the church functions well, there is nothing like it. Other organizations may accomplish lofty goals and, therefore, experience the satisfaction of knowing they have reached their goals. But the church has the added joy of knowing they have done what God has given them to do. Typically, when a congregation reassembles on the Sunday after Operation Inasmuch, it is a special time of celebration and thanksgiving. Such was the case at St. James.

From the moment people arrived at church, you heard a buzz of sharing about the experiences of the previous day— telling about what they did in Operation Inasmuch, sharing about the persons to whom they ministered, moaning over the parts of their bodies that hurt from manual labor, and celebrating the wonder of how much could be done in just one day. The congregants of St. James gathered around the bulletin board in the church hallway to view the pictures from the previous day, looking for themselves but also viewing the many projects accomplished by their church. One person exclaimed: "I can't believe this is my church!"

This is why it is important that a church include in their planning for their first Operation Inasmuch a time to celebrate, usually in worship the following day while the experience is still fresh. Most persons are immersed in their own project and do not get the full effect of the entire Operation Inasmuch unless there is a time for sharing. At St. James the morning worship services were given to a celebration of God's work in them through Operation Inasmuch.

The pastor encouraged volunteers to share from their experiences of the previous day. A woman in her sixties said Operation Inasmuch was one of the greatest things St. James has done, so productive and providing so much fellowship. A middle-aged man said that what struck him was how many of their congregation came together to help so many others. Another man, who worked on the home repair project in the same neighborhood where a couple of dozen other such projects were going on at the same time, said he was impressed that so many different denominations of churches put aside their differences to do God's work.

Some of the sharing offered spiritual insights. Pastor Hilbert kept her remarks brief so as to allow as much time as possible for others to tell their stories. However, her observations offered deeper reflections that added to the meaning of the experience for the entire church. She told of visiting with the woman whose home was repaired. The woman told her that she had been praying for the money to get the work done, and a few days later someone came to her door and asked if they could fix her house for her. She is convinced God sent the caller and the volunteers from St. James who did the work as an answer to her prayers.

The comments of a woman named Stella were especially meaningful. She said she realized Sunday morning that she had felt God's presence at St. James during Operation Inasmuch. She worked on the quilt project and, therefore, was in a separate room most of the day. When she came out of the room and saw so many people working together, she wondered if that is what heaven is like. Another *kairos* moment had occurred in another congregation through Operation Inasmuch.

Evaluating the Experience

The above celebrations notwithstanding, it is essential that the group responsible for the planning and execution of an Operation Inasmuch meet to evaluate the experience. This evaluation should take place within two weeks of the event, while observations and thoughts are still fresh. It is natural that the intensity of the planning and the excitement of the event and subsequent celebration will bring on a letdown in emotion—all the more reason for the coordinator to schedule this evaluation immediately.

In the case of St. James, the coordinator shared the numbers of their Operation Inasmuch—how many people involved, how many touched by some ministry, how many of this and that giving the full scope of what they had accomplished. She guided her committee through an assessment of each of the projects. Overall, the assessment was extremely positive. Some offered suggestions as to how some of the projects could be better. For example, some of the volunteers in the wheelchair project were under-utilized as the supervisors from the Council on Older Adults (the community agency that arranged for the wheelchair ramp projects) did more working than supervising. It was noted that better communication between project leaders and volunteers prior to the day of Operation Inasmuch was needed. More information about the projects needed to be shared during the sign-up phase, and they needed more projects even for the same number of people and especially if more get involved. Although photos were taken of all the activities, a video account would have been a valuable historical reference and promotional tool in the future.

None of these suggestions were viewed as negatives. The overwhelming consensus agreed that St. James should do Operation Inasmuch again. Some of the comments of the group were telling: "I doubt that anyone who was helped during Operation Inasmuch got more from it than we did." "I've been going to this church for fifty years, and I've never seen as many people excited or as much adrenaline flowing as I saw last Saturday." "I finally saw what Pastor Louise has been harping about in discipleship! It was demonstrated in Operation Inasmuch."

St. James Lutheran Church has now joined the ranks of hundreds of other congregations in becoming a mission outpost in their community. There is no turning back now. Once they have tasted of the sweet joy of being used by God to make a difference in their community, they can never go back to "church as usual." All of which is to say that a few more saints have been melted down and put into circulation.

What about your church? Are you looking for something to energize and mobilize your congregation in hands-on ministry? Do any of the stories of churches' experiences with Operation Inasmuch make you wish you could see the same happen in your church? Then do it. Take the leap. Transform your church into a mission outpost for your community.

The Web site www.operationinasmuch.com is available as a source of current information about churches signing on to this exciting way of doing local mission work and as a clearinghouse for new ideas of how to be more creative and effective in conducting an Operation Inasmuch. If you want to learn more about other churches' experiences or get more ideas about projects, log on to the site and glean from the wealth of information there. Also, please register there when your church conducts your first Operation Inasmuch. We would like to build a network of Operation Inasmuch churches throughout the country, learning from one another and helping one another get better and better at being the hands and feet of Jesus to a hurting world.

10

The Multi-church Experience

First Baptist Church, Murfreesboro, Tennessee, conducted their first Operation Inasmuch in March 2004.[1] They had three hundred volunteers (out of an average attendance of about five hundred) carry out thirty projects. When members of neighbor churches read of the impact of Operation Inasmuch on their community, they contacted Kristina Brown, director of volunteer ministries at First Baptist, and asked if she would share the concept with them. As of the writing of this chapter, First Baptist is planning to partner with Episcopal, Presbyterian, and Christian congregations in Murfreesboro to conduct their second Operation Inasmuch, an interdenominational blitz into their community in October 2004. They are planning for upwards of five hundred volunteers on as many as fifty projects. More people in Murfreesboro will receive some of the help they need. More church folk will discover the joy of giving themselves to minister to others in nontraditional ways, as well as the satisfaction of chipping away at the barriers between denominations. The church—not just a single congregation, but *the* body of Christ in that community—will earn a greater share of the community's respect, all because of Operation Inasmuch.

This is the way a multi-church Operation Inasmuch often happens. A church conducts an Operation Inasmuch, and the word gets out about their positive experience. Members of that congregation share with friends in other congregations in their community about their experience. One thing leads to another until the first congregation is sharing with others in their community how to do Operation Inasmuch. Or they invite other congregations to join them in conducting an Operation Inasmuch.

In this final chapter, I will address the multi-church Operation Inasmuch. I will share the advantages of this approach and give a step-by-step guide for planning and implementing a multi-church experience. It should be noted that partnering to do Operation Inasmuch is not necessarily confined to churches. While it is recommended that it *always* be a ministry with clear groundings in Matthew 25, it is possible to expand involvement into community organizations. For example, at the writing of this chapter, I am preparing to share with my Rotary Club (at their invitation) how they might become involved in our next Operation Inasmuch regardless of whether they are members of any of the churches represented.

As I mentioned earlier, Snyder Memorial Baptist Church recognized the potential of Operation Inasmuch to strengthen their relationship with believers of other races and congregations back in 1997. I had met with Dr. Cureton Johnson, pastor of First Baptist Church, Moore Street, in Fayetteville, an African American congregation, and discussed the possibility of our churches working together in an Operation Inasmuch. I had proposed that we plan together, pool our resources, and assign volunteers from both congregations for all projects. He agreed that this could promote stronger fellowship between our churches as well as meet a larger set of needs in the community. When the two congregations met together to kick off the joint Operation Inasmuch, it was a beautiful sight—black and white believers seated together, preparing together to work together for the day. It was the most significant advance in race relations that had ever taken place between those two churches.

But it was just the beginning. Word of that experience spread throughout Fayetteville. Congregational leaders began to inquire as to how they might learn more about Operation Inasmuch. The minister of missions and lay ministries at Snyder Memorial regularly responded to requests that she come to other churches and tell the Operation Inasmuch story. One by one, congregations joined the parade of churches getting outside the walls of their buildings to minister to the human hurts and hopes of Fayetteville. Today, about thirty-five congregations participate in Operation Inasmuch there twice a year. Hence, the impact this ministry has had on the larger community as described in the first chapter of this book.

Many churches have found that sharing Operation Inasmuch with other churches in their community, especially inviting them actually to share in the experience, is a natural development from the successes of their own event. It is human nature to want to share a good experience with friends. When those friends attend other churches, it often leads to a shared Operation Inasmuch. That sharing may take the form of simply telling what Operation Inasmuch is and how to implement it. The new church may then plan and conduct their own Operation Inasmuch independent of other churches.

Such has been the experience in Tallahassee, Florida. In November of 2003, First Baptist Church of Tallahassee conducted their "First Love" event. (They chose to adapt the name of their event to fit their church and to be consistent with the names of other First Baptist events throughout the year, but they followed the Operation Inasmuch plan completely.) Soon afterward, an Episcopal church in Tallahassee called Tom Perrin, First Baptist's coordinator of First Love, and asked if he would teach them how to do an Operation Inasmuch. In the fall of 2004 the Episcopal church held their first Operation Inasmuch as a stand-alone event.

Without a doubt, the most ambitious multi-church effort at Operation Inasmuch has been led by Wendy Edwards, regional coordinator of the Baptist State Convention of North Carolina. Wendy resources two hundred fifty Baptist congregations in a nine county region of northeastern North Carolina. She recognized Operation Inasmuch as a tool to mobilize Baptists in her area more effectively. She provided training in what Operation Inasmuch is and how it could empower churches to do a better job of ministering to local needs using the initial materials developed by Snyder Memorial Baptist Church. Fifty congregations conducted Operation Inasmuch projects initially. That was in the late 1990s. Today there are about one hundred twenty-five churches participating.

Because these churches cover such a large geographical area, Wendy and her leadership team have recommended a date for all the congregations to hold Operation Inasmuch. Some of the smaller churches conduct only one or two projects, while larger churches do more. The churches plan and work independently of each other, but on the same day, making a huge impact on their area of the state. Edwards says: "Operation Inasmuch is one of the best things we do in our area. Spin-off ministries have developed from it, one of which is a team to build wheelchair ramps with a government agency throughout the year."

The More the Merrier

If one church can make a lasting difference in its community through Operation Inasmuch, two or more churches working together can broaden the impact. The most conspicuous advantage of the multi-church Operation Inasmuch is an increase in projects and volunteers. In our largest Operation Inasmuch at Central Baptist Church of Fountain City (Knoxville, Tenn.), we had five hundred volunteers conducting about forty projects. When we involved members of Fountain City Presbyterian Church and St. Paul United Methodist Church, we had seven hundred fifty volunteers doing sixty projects. Many more people in the community were served, and more believers experienced the joy of serving. And it continues to grow. As of the writing of this chapter, five churches in the Fountain City area are making plans for a multi-church Operation Inasmuch in the fall of 2004 that will involve approximately eight hundred volunteers doing seventy projects.

The primary benefit of a multi-church Operation Inasmuch to the churches involved is the enhanced fellowship among the congregations. It is a sad fact of church life that congregations rarely work together until there is a controversial political issue that supersedes their individual ministries and the competition that often characterizes inter-church relationships. Almost anything that breaks through the artificial barriers between congregations, especially between denominations, is seen as impressive. And when that breakthrough event is authentic ministry in the name of Jesus given to people who truly need the help, it verges on miraculous.

Pam Eubanks has had the unique opportunity to see a church move from a one-church event to a multi-church experience. She worked on Operation Inasmuch for Central Baptist Church of Fountain City in their initial two events, then moved on to Fountain City Presbyterian Church, which became one of three churches in the spring of 2004 Operation Inasmuch. This is her assessment of that experience:

> That day, adorned in our blue Operation Inasmuch T-shirts, we were all alike serving Christ through serving the least of these. I was reminded of Jesus' prayer for us to be "One" as he and God are "One." There is nothing comparable to development of the "tie that binds" a group of diverse church families than that of Operation Inasmuch. Petty differences always diminish in the commitment to and understanding of our call to serve Christ. What an exciting vision of the Kingdom of God on earth![2]

Inviting other congregations to join in conducting an Operation Inasmuch renews that church's enthusiasm for this sort of ministry. I have been a pastor for more than two decades, so I have seen plenty of promising ministries come and go. Everything loses its luster after a while. It is virtually impossible to maintain the enthusiasm of a new ministry indefinitely without introducing new dimensions to it. This is what a multi-church Operation Inasmuch does. Adding other churches, enlarging the number of volunteers and projects, and teaching others how to do it add new life to Operation Inasmuch. It's simply the next step after a few successes. Kathy Rosenbalm, Operation Inasmuch coordinator for Central Baptist of Fountain City, says:

> Teaming with other churches keeps the excitement alive. Experiencing Operation Inasmuch for the first time is a very exciting experience in part because it is a new way to reach out to others and a new way to serve God. After the first time, it is still exciting and fun, but not like the first time when it was all shiny and new. Teaming with other churches provides the opportunity to relive that first-time excitement through their experience.[3]

Martha Johnson served as the coordinator of Central Baptist's first attempt to partner with other congregations in Operation Inasmuch. At first, she felt intimidated by the challenge of identifying enough projects to enable 50 percent more volunteers to have a positive experience. However, she discovered that broader participation actually helped. She says:

> The resource opportunities grew by amazing proportions. Each time we added new churches we encountered folk with different gifts and skills. We found many new community contacts, opening more opportunities for service. It has strengthened our community.[4]

How to Conduct a Multi-church Operation Inasmuch

I am often asked whether it is better for a church to conduct its first Operation Inasmuch alone or partner with a neighbor congregation. While it is not impossible to conduct a multi-church Operation Inasmuch initially, it makes more sense for a church to learn "the ropes" of this complex ministry before trying to guide another congregation through the experience. No matter how thorough planning may be, some things cannot be learned except by experience. I recommend that a church do possibly two Operation Inasmuch events before bringing in another congregation with them. Then, share it aggressively!

The planning process is essentially the same in a multi-church experience as in a stand-alone event. The same steps described in chapter 8 should be followed in the multi-church experience.

Share the Story

The multi-church experience begins with a meeting involving the Operation Inasmuch leadership team of the church that has conducted one or more events (hereafter referred to as the lead church) and the corresponding team of another congregation. A significant portion of this meeting should be given to storytelling, i.e., sharing the lead church's experience with Operation Inasmuch—what it did for the congregation, what it did for individual participants, and its impact on the community. The material emphasized in chapters 2 and 3 of this book provides a workable outline for this sharing, with—of course—personal, local stories substituted for those presented in the book. Hopefully, the lead church compiled photos of their Operation Inasmuch into a PowerPoint™ presentation, or recorded it in a well-done video, as some form of visual record will best communicate their story to those who are just learning about it. (A video of a multi-church experience by Central Baptist Church of Fountain City, Knoxville, Tenn., [my current church] is available on the DVD that comes with this book. A PowerPoint™ presentation is also on the DVD in the "Support Materials" portion of the DVD. The points of the presentation correspond to the points in chapters 2 and 3.)

Set the Date

Predictably, response to this sharing will be excitement and eagerness to get to work planning a multi-church Operation Inasmuch. The first item of business will be to set a date. The lead church may have already set the date of their next Operation Inasmuch and may simply invite the other congregation(s) to join them. If those congregations have no conflicts on their calendars, this date may be satisfactory to all. Conversation between congregational leaders prior to this initial meeting may also provide ample opportunity to clear a date that is satisfactory to all of the churches involved. Although we stated this earlier, it bears repeating here: The date of Operation Inasmuch should not conflict with major community events, e.g., local college football games, the county fair, seasonal festivals, or any event that tends to draw significant participation from the entire community. The more churches who partner together, the more this rule applies.

The date of Operation Inasmuch should allow sufficient time for thorough planning and preparation. We recommend that this date be approximately four months after the initial meeting. Adequate preparations may be made with a shorter time line, but the leadership team will need to keep in mind that each step of the process will be new to those for whom Operation Inasmuch is still new. Members of the team from the lead church can move more quickly through the process, but newcomers to the process will face a steeper learning curve. Remembering that this is essentially a teaching venue will encourage patience.

Set the Leadership Team

If the persons present at the initial meeting of the multi-church leadership team are not those who will actually plan and implement Operation Inasmuch, the group will need to decide who those persons will be. They may be an ad hoc group selected by appropriate means by the participating churches or, as usually happens, they may be a standing committee or group, e.g., the missions committee. However each church's members of the leadership team are selected, they should be dependable, motivated, self-starting, creative persons. They must have sufficient respect within their congregation to be able to "sell" Operation Inasmuch to them. It is helpful if some of them are already actively involved in local ministries beyond their own church, say, volunteers in local benevolent agencies. Their knowledge of those agencies may prove very helpful when it comes to developing sufficient projects for a multi-church Operation Inasmuch. The committee members should have a thorough knowledge of their congregations' gifts, strengths, skills, resources, facilities, and ability to work with others.

A word about pastoral leaders is appropriate here. It is important that the pastor of any church considering undertaking Operation Inasmuch be on board with the effort. He or she needs to support it publicly and to volunteer to serve on one of the projects. Pastoral support makes a huge difference in how responsive a congregation is to the challenges of doing Operation Inasmuch. In the multi-church events I have observed personally where the pastor is not personally involved, the churches almost always have a lower rate of congregational involvement. The pastor does not have to be present in the planning sessions or take any other responsibility for the effort, but the pastor of every church must choose a project to get involved in and tell the church about that project and the pastor's involvement. The pastor must also support the committee's work and personally praise and support the committee before the congregation.

Brainstorm Projects

The leadership team may begin brainstorming potential projects for the multi-church Operation Inasmuch. At this point in the process, the team will want to identify all possible ideas without making judgments as to their viability. This is free-wheeling brainstorming. Participants are encouraged to "lay on the table" everything their churches are already doing in the way of ministry beyond the boundaries of their campuses.

Normally, once this brainstorming begins, it gathers momentum for a time, with plenty of ideas surfacing.

An excellent starting point for this part of the process will be those projects the lead church has conducted in their Operation Inasmuch. By this time they know what has worked well and should be prepared to offer those proven projects. Another source of project ideas is the Operation Inasmuch Web site (www.operationinasmuch.com), where fresh stories are regularly reported, including some of the projects conducted.

Refine the Projects

The brainstorming of projects may consume several meetings of the multi-church leadership team. Fairly early in this process, the team will need to evaluate the viability of project ideas. The same criteria for those projects mentioned in chapter 8 apply. Of course, more projects will be required for a multi-church event because you will have more volunteers. A good rule of thumb is that you should plan enough projects to involve 50 to 75 percent of each congregation's average Sunday morning attendance. For example, if Church A averages 400 in attendance, Church B 200, and Church C 150, the combined number of volunteers could be between 375 and 562. Admittedly, this is a wide range, but most of the projects will have some flexibility as to how many volunteers can be utilized in them, and, therefore, will accommodate a fairly wide target number of volunteers. Another way to be confident that adequate projects are planned is to target a slightly lower number of volunteers, say 50 percent of average attendances, then plan a few additional projects that are not promoted initially. If the response is higher than expected, put these additional projects into play.

If child care and ministry to homebound members of each church are included as projects in the multi-church event, it is best that these be planned for each church to do on their own. For example, since preschool children are more comfortable in a facility with which they are familiar, it is best that Church A provide child care for children from that church, staffing it with volunteers from that church, and the same for Church B, and so on. Also, each church will want to organize ministry to its own homebound, utilizing members of that church to visit homebound members.

Recruit Project Leaders

Once sufficient projects have been planned, the committee needs to recruit project leaders. Again, some of the project leaders from the lead church will be available. However, care should be taken to recruit project leaders from the new congregations. The best way for a church to get up to speed on Operation Inasmuch is for members to have the responsibilities of project leaders. Another approach to this recruitment process is to enlist co-leaders. Where possible, one leader may be from the lead church with experience in managing an Operation Inasmuch project, and another from a new congregation in a sort of mentoring arrangement. I have seen this approach work well.

Of course, it is essential that project leaders understand what they are agreeing to do, what their responsibilities are:

- Prepare for their project, including the acquisition of appropriate materials
- Contact every volunteer on their project and communicate the nature of the project and any information the volunteers may need to have a satisfying experience
- Lead in executing the project on the day of Operation Inasmuch
- Provide feedback to the coordinator and/or leadership team, which will enhance future events

Considerations Unique to the Multi-church Experience

When a congregation decides to share Operation Inasmuch with other congregations, the lead church faces the danger of adopting a bit of a hierarchical attitude, such as, "We know how to do this, so watch and listen to us." The lead church that conveys this attitude will surely meet with some resistance or perhaps a lack of cooperation. I cannot stress enough that the lead church needs to "go the extra mile" to avoid any condescension or sense of superiority. Most often a person from the lead church, probably that church's Operation Inasmuch coordinator, will preside at the multi-church planning meetings. Experience is the key. However, this can be done in a way that involves and values every church, every person, and every idea.

One way of making sure the field is level for everyone is to rotate the meetings among the churches involved. Hosting a meeting seems to encourage a deeper buy-in by those who are new to the process. Another way of accomplishing a healthy sense of cooperation and equality is to plan projects that take place in each church's facilities. Those projects that take place in church buildings can be shared among the participating churches. Logos or materials (e.g., sign-up forms) should not bear the name of an individual church, former project leader, etc. Finally, leadership for the kick-off gathering on Saturday morning and any celebration following Operation Inasmuch should be shared by persons from all of the participating churches. I usually ask ministers from other churches to give the devotional challenge to the participants and/or to lead in music in the kickoff gathering, as well as lead in some way at the celebration event.

Another way of fostering a greater sense of "we're all in this together" is to have T-shirts available that volunteers may purchase. Most communities have a source where T-shirts designed for a specific event can be produced at a reasonable price. The T-shirt used in the Knoxville multi-church Operation Inasmuch has the OIAM logo on the front and Matthew 25:40 on the back. (*Note:* If you have T-shirts made, leave off the date so they can be worn for future events.) When volunteers from several churches are sporting the same T-shirt, it tends to unify the group. (The OIAM logo is available on the accompanying DVD.)

The cost of a multi-church event should be shared fairly. In Knoxville, what has worked well is that the lead church initially bears the total expense of the event, with project leaders reporting all their expenses. Once it is known how many volunteers from each church have participated, the percentage of the total number is determined. Then each congregation pays that percentage of the total costs.

The kickoff gathering on Saturday morning and the post–Operation Inasmuch celebration become even more significant in a multi-church experience. Since one of the primary reasons for holding such an event is fostering closer fellowship among the participating churches, not to gather all the volunteers from those churches together would waste the opportunity to experience one of the most joyous events in any church's life. My experience is that these are some the happiest, most memorable events ever.

The coordinators have some important business to attend to on the morning of the kickoff event besides making sure all volunteers know where they are to go and what they are to do. Sharing cell phone numbers with each project leader enables better communication throughout the day. These coordinators will want to have decided prior to the kickoff event how they will divide up responsibilities. For example, one or two will need to remain at the "command central" location in order to respond to needs that arise throughout the day. Perhaps one of them, or another member of the leadership team, will serve as a host or hostess for members of other churches who may be on hand to observe Operation Inasmuch. Another may be assigned to serve as a guide for media representatives. There is plenty of work for everyone to do, and dividing it appropriately will help everything run more smoothly.

The post–Operation Inasmuch celebration is valuable for another reason. Volunteers know about their own projects and perhaps a few others, but are not able to get the full scope of Operation Inasmuch's impact on their community unless they hear and see reports from others. The full impact of what churches working together have accomplished is best experienced in these celebrations. Usually the best way to report the results of Operation Inasmuch is to have a person from the leadership team report the numbers, such as volunteers, projects, projects' results, etc. Volunteers sharing what they did in Operation Inasmuch and what it meant to them is the most meaningful part of these celebrations. Finally, it may be possible to have a recipient of something done in one or more of the projects present to share from his or her perspective.

The Zebulon Story

One of the most moving stories of a multi-church experience comes out of Zebulon, North Carolina. Zebulon is a small but rapidly growing community a few miles north of Raleigh. Zebulon Baptist Church began doing Operation Inasmuch in the late 1990s. References to their experiences occur in previous chapters of this book. In their Operation Inasmuch, they invited an African American congregation in Zebulon to join with them. They have continued to do Operation Inasmuch together each year. Jack Glasgow, pastor of Zebulon Baptist Church, reports that a Zebulon city councilman has said publicly that Operation Inasmuch has done more for race relations than anything else that has happened in their community.

In one of their post–Operation Inasmuch celebrations, persons from both congregations were sharing about their experiences the previous day. One woman stood and related a story of something that happened in her family in prior generations, the effects of which were still felt by her and other members of her family, causing resentment toward white people to simmer for generations. When she spoke in the joint celebration of Operation Inasmuch, she talked about the power of working with fellow believers from another church, a white church, to help her heal from the emotional wounds she carried for a long time. She said, "It took me putting on work clothes and gloves and getting down on my hands and knees working alongside some of the people of this church (Zebulon Baptist) to begin to release the anger I've felt for years because of what happened in my family."

As powerful as that is, the story doesn't end there. Some time later a descendant of the white man involved in the original act of violence died. He was a member of Zebulon Baptist Church. His family invited the black woman and her family to sit with them at his funeral, advancing the healing that began earlier with Operation Inasmuch—all because two churches used Operation Inasmuch as a way to work together to meet some of the practical needs of the people in their community.

Sample Operation Inasmuch Projects

Backyard Bible Club—Gathering of children from a neighborhood for games, entertainment (e.g., puppets), and Bible stories. Excellent project for teenagers.

Sewing Projects—Blankets for homeless persons. Turbans for cancer patients. Walker bags for nursing home patients. Stuffed animals to be given by police to abused children.

Home Repairs—Plumbing, electrical, roofing, painting, repair of windows, porches, steps, rotting exteriors, etc. Some, but not all, participants will need specialized skills. Needs identified by local community agencies or elderly church members.

Wheelchair Ramps—Construction of wheelchair ramp either in partnership with local agency that provides this service to elderly and/or disabled persons, or as a stand-alone project by the church. Some building codes may be applicable.

Homebound Visitation—Personal visits to all persons in the church's homebound ministry. It is helpful for visitors to take something to leave with homebound persons, e.g., a flower, small gift, etc.

Life Books for Foster Children—Assembly of notebooks to be given to foster children by local Department of Social Services, in which the children will keep pictures, notes, letters, newspaper clippings, or other items that will help them retain significant memories.

Yard Work for Elderly/Disabled Persons—Seasonal, light cleanup and maintenance for persons unable to do or provide for themselves.

Blood Pressure Checkups—Multiple, public locations—malls, grocery stores, shopping centers, fire stations, etc. It is helpful to include an appropriate handout that provides hints for good health and/or low-key spiritual guidance.

Affirmation of Public Servants—Deliver appropriate expressions of gratitude and concern (cookies, Bible or other literature, flowers, etc.) to local police, fire, emergency, and health personnel.

Packaging of Foods at Food Bank—Division of large quantities of nonperishable food items (potatoes, cheese, etc.) into smaller quantities to be distributed by local food bank.

Mountain of Potatoes—Obtain a truckload of potatoes or other local, surplus agricultural product and have volunteers package them in smaller quantities to be distributed locally.

Firewood Cutting and Delivery—Cut firewood and deliver to persons identified by local agencies who heat with wood.

Care for Care-Givers—Prepare and deliver a 30–day devotional guide to encourage persons who work in the challenging environments of nursing homes, retirement homes, and/or hospitals.

Lunch Preparation and Delivery—Prepare and deliver light lunch for all volunteers.

Baby Shower for Maternity Home—Conduct a baby shower for expectant mothers at local maternity home.

Assembly Projects—Assembly of packages such as hygiene kits for homeless persons, Easter baskets for children of poverty, stuffed animals for abused children, etc., usually conducted in church facilities and distributed at a later date.

Clothing/Food Collection—Collection of clothing and/or nonperishable food items to be delivered to local agencies for distribution or for church's Clothes Closet or Food Bank.

Love Lunches—Preparation and distribution of lunches at local Salvation Army or homeless shelter.

Smoke Alarms—Installation of smoke alarms in low-income housing in partnership with local agency or fire prevention program.

Rest Stop Ministry—Provide coffee and/or soft drinks, local information, and friendly greeting at area highway welcome station or rest stop.

Ministry Training—Train persons willing to become involved in local caring ministries such as Hospice, Contact, Adult Literacy, Teen Mentoring, etc.

Garden Project—Plant a garden for low-income family and provide know-how for continued care.

Writing Letters to Prisoners—Write letters to local or area prisoners and correctional staff encouraging them and offering appropriate spiritual guidance. *Note:* Be sure to follow guidelines for such letters required by local correctional institutions.

Block Party—Provide lunch, entertainment, and basic services at housing project or in an area where other projects are concentrated (several home repair projects). Usually local agencies will provide limited services or information concerning their services. This project can be conducted at a church near a depressed neighborhood as an outreach into that neighborhood.

Nursing Home Ministry—Using music personnel, provide entertaining and inspirational program at local nursing homes.

Vaccination/Health Clinic—Using health professionals, offer vaccinations and health screenings in neighborhoods where these services are not available. If a mobile health facility such as a medical/dental bus is available, it may be the center of such a project.

Child Care—Provide child care in church facilities for families with young children to facilitate their participation in other projects.

Blood Drive—Conduct a blood drive in conjunction with local blood assurance agency.

Prayer Project—Three prayer projects: (1) have volunteers pray before and during Operation Inasmuch for its effectiveness, (2) set up a prayer tent in a neighborhood (usually in conjunction with other projects in the same neighborhood) to receive requests from locals, and (3) do a prayer walk around local schools or OIAM projects.

APPENDIX B

Sample Operation Inasmuch (OIAM) Sign-up Sheet

Name_____ Phone_____

Check the project(s) you want to be part of on _____.
Prayer team and blood drive participants will have time to be part of another project as well.

___ Child care provider (for OIAM participants)
___ Building wheelchair ramps
___ City Rescue Mission work (details not yet finalized)
___ Assembly project (assembling Easter baskets and/or health care kits)
___ Blood donor
___ Assist with signing up donors
___ Lunch preparation and delivery (lunch for all participants)
___ Will donate blood
___ Prayer team
___ Quilt making and tying
___ Home repair project
___ Visiting with sick and homebound
___ Yard cleanup
___ Block party (held where home repair project is)
___ Baby shower for unwed mothers

Please list your skills:

___ Blood pressure checks (taking BP readings for others)	___ Sewing
___ Carpentry	___ Roofing
___ Plumbing	___ Painting
___ Electrical	___ Other (_____)

Child care needed:

Name_____ Age_____

Name_____ Age_____

Name_____ Age_____

Return this sheet: To the church office, in offering plate, *or* send to OIAM director's name and address.

QUESTIONS???—call xxx-xxxx

Sample Operation Inasmuch
Master Teams List

On the next page is the first page of a Master Team List from an actual Operation Inasmuch. The OIAM coordinator can use such a master list to see who's working on what and where more workers are needed. It also may be sent to project leaders for their use in making reminder calls to volunteers and would be helpful if organizers had to locate a volunteer quickly on the day of the event. It may also be used in evaluating the event and planning for the next one. For many reasons, it is good to have all volunteers' names and where they're working available in one document.

Sample Operation Inasmuch Master Teams List

Project Number & Name	Team Leader Name & Phone Number	# Volunteers Needed	Volunteers Name & Phone Number	Description & Comments
PROJECT 1 Child Care		4		Children up to 3rd grade. 8 a.m. until 2 p.m. Alyson & David Wood providing snacks + drinks. Can use things from Sun. school office for crafts.
PROJECT 2 Assembly Project		20		Easter baskets for children at T.C. Berrien & Pauline Jones Elementary Schools. Lee will help Sharon coordinate and purchase items for the baskets.
PROJECT 3 Lunches		10		Lunch preparation & delivery for St. James' participants + for families having homes repaired, painted, ramp built or yards cleaned. Project leaders will need to call church with number of lunches needed when they first arrive at project site.

Sample Operation Inasmuch Checklist for Calls to Church Members

(OIAM is on March 17 in this example)

Week of March 5

1. Ask if they know about Operation Inasmuch from the Temple talks and "The Messenger."
2. If they say no—tell them about it and ask them to sign up! Go over the various projects on the Project List. The Baby Shower project has been added (see Project List). We will be building one wheelchair ramp through coordination with Council on Older Adults. We will be participating in the Block Party that is held for the children in the neighborhood where the homes are being repaired.
3. If they say yes—thank them! Ask if everyone in the family has signed up, including children older than the third grade.
4. Once they've signed up (previously or during your call), ask if they need child care for any child up to third grade. If yes, get names and ages of the children. Child care will be offered between 8 a.m. and 2 p.m., at the church. Mid-morning snacks will be provided.
5. Encourage any donations of money or materials. Any check should be made out to St. James, with Operation Inasmuch on the memo line. Materials specifically needed are:
   • Any new or nice used baby things for the Baby Shower.
   • Bud vases for the Visitation Project.
   • Sample-size toiletries for the Health Care Kits for the homeless.

- Candy for Easter baskets for children
- Canned soft drinks & single-serving size potato chip bags for the Block Party.

6. Remind them that there will be a blood drive in St. James's parking lot between 1:00 p.m. and 5:00 p.m. Encourage people to sign up now to donate so the blood donor center can plan for sufficient help.

7. Remind them that on March 17, our day will begin at 8:00 a.m., with a short worship service in the sanctuary. From there, we will disperse to our different projects.

8. Ask for their prayers for our March 17 Operation Inasmuch.

Sample Operation Inasmuch
First Letter to Project Leaders

March 1

Dear Operation Inasmuch Project Leaders,

Thank you all so much for your willingness to take on these projects! We have not had much planning time for this Operation Inasmuch, but have already accomplished a lot. As of today, we've had fifty-four people sign up for various projects and know that more will sign up in the next one to two weeks. Below is a list of things you all need to know.

- You will need to call the volunteers for your project after March 11, preferably three or four days prior to March 17, to remind them to show up on March 17 and to give them any project specifics. We've had quite a few people sign up for two or more projects, telling us to put them where they are most needed. Next week I will put these people on the projects where we need them and will then send you an updated master list.
- For all projects done away from the church, it would be helpful if you have a cell phone available. If you don't have one, we can supposedly borrow some from Sun Com or Alltel. Please let me know your cell phone number or if we need to try to get you a phone to use March 17.
- St. James's insurance carrier has been contacted about Operation Inasmuch. *If* we have any injuries, I will call them.

- Our next Operation Inasmuch planning meeting is Tuesday, March 6 at 7:30 p.m. You are very welcome to attend if you want to and can. I will send you the meeting report if you are unable to attend.
- On March 17, we will have a short "kickoff" worship service in our sanctuary at 8:00 a.m. From there, we will disperse to our different projects. Please plan to attend this service with your project's other volunteers.
- If you have volunteers for your project that are not on the enclosed master list, please let me know their names. We are trying to keep a master list of everyone participating in some way in Operation Inasmuch.
- Sack lunches will be provided on March 17. Anyone working at the church will get lunch there. Lunches will be delivered to anyone working on projects away from the church. When you first arrive at your project site March 17, we will need you to call the church with the number of lunches you will need. Please include the St. James volunteers plus family members of the homes you may be working on.
- Within the next week you should know the details of your project—the specifics of what you will be doing and any materials you need. If there's anything I can help you with, please let me know.
- I am the central contact person for our Operation Inasmuch. I will contact you with any late sign-ups or any last-minute information I may learn. Call me if you need anything!

Thank you again.
We have truly been blessed in this opportunity.

Name of Coordinator
Phone number
E-mail address

Sample Operation Inasmuch
Final Letter to Project Leaders

March 13

Dear Operation Inasmuch Project Leaders,

March 17 is fast approaching, and it's going to be a truly wonderful day! We have 126 people signed up to participate in our Operation Inasmuch!! I wanted to send you some last-minute thoughts...

- Remember our 8:00 a.m. worship service in the sanctuary and please ask the volunteers on your team to attend that service if at all possible. It will be short and from there, we will disperse to our separate projects.
- *If* it rains Saturday, you will need to be the contact person for your team. If it rains, we will still do the projects that take place at the church. We would hope to be able to do the outdoor projects, too, but it will be up to you. You may need to let your team members know whether the projects are going to take place or not if we wake up to rain Saturday morning. The projects coordinated through the Fayetteville Urban Ministry or Council on Older Adults would need to coordinate with those agencies if we have rain. But—of course, it isn't going to rain because we've all prayed for good weather all week!!!
- For the projects away from the church: You will need to bring coolers full of ice with you to your project site if

you want ice for your sodas. There won't be any ice brought with the lunches.

- Please keep records of any expenses you've incurred for your project. I'm keeping records of what we spend for the different projects so that our next Operation Inasmuch planning will be easier. For reimbursement of any expenses, Judy needs receipts plus completion of the reimbursement form. If you don't have a copy of this form, you can get one from Judy or from me.
- *Remember* to call the church (484–XXXX) after you get to your project site, with the number of lunches you will need. We plan to provide lunch for any family members of the homes you are working on, unless they would rather fix their own lunches. Barbara Reich, lunch team leader, will need the total number of lunches you need, including those for volunteers *and* family members.
- *If* you complete your project and any on your team wish to help with other projects, call me at the church. *Or* if you need additional help, call me and we'll send any extra volunteers to you.
- After your project is completed on Saturday, please call me at the church with the number of volunteers you had working and how much you accomplished. For example, I want to know how many walker bags and Easter baskets and quilts we make Saturday.

Again, thank you so much for all the work and planning you've done for Operation Inasmuch!

Name of Coordinator
Phone number
E-mail address

Notes

Chapter 1: Circulating the Saints

[1]Esther Burroughs, *Empowered: Reclaiming the Meaning of Missions Through the Power of the Holy Spirit* (Birmingham, Ala.: Women's Missionary Union, 1990), 49.

[2]Edward H. Hammett, *The Gathered and Scattered Church: Equipping Believers for the 21st Century* (Macon, Ga. : Smyth & Helwys, 1999), 22.

[3]National Civic League, "The All-America City Award," 2000.

[4]Letter from Julia Scatliff-O'Grady and Diana Jones-Wilson, co-chairs of the Governor's Summit on America's Promise and Volunteerism, March 3, 1998.

[5]Burroughs, *Empowered,* 56.

Chapter 2: Transforming Believers and Congregations

[1]Interview with Jay Gilbert, First Presbyterian Church, Fayetteville, N.C., March, 8, 2000.

[2]Frank Newport, "The Fascinating 'Local Versus National' Phenomenon," The Gallup Organization, http://www.gallup.com/poll/fromtheed/ed0102.asp>.

[3]Interview with Vicky Perry, Winter Park Baptist Church, Wilmington, N.C., February 24, 2001.

[4]E-mail to author from Jackie Strickland, Zebulon Baptist Church, Zebulon, N.C., n.d.

[5]Interview with Ruth Smith, First Baptist Church, Fayetteville, N.C., February 6, 2001.

[6]Interview with Jay Gilbert.

[7]Interview with Mary Poole, First Baptist Church, Clinton, N.C., February 7, 2000.

[8]Interview with Vicky Perry.

[9]Interview with Greg Miller, Lafayette Baptist Church, Fayetteville, N.C., March 15, 2000.

[10]Interview with Dave Davis, Holy Trinity Episcopal Church, Fayetteville, N.C., February 7, 2001.

[11]Letter from Debby McBride, First Baptist Church, Monroe, N.C., n.d.

[12]Interview with Greg Miller.

[13]Interview with Archie Pierce, Beverly Hills Baptist Church, Asheville, N.C., February 21, 2001.

[14]E-mail to author from Nancy Sears, Pleasant Grove Baptist Church, Fuquay-Varina, N.C., 12 February 2001.

[15]Interview with Jim Fowler, Ardmore Baptist Church, Winston-Salem, N.C., January 25, 2000.

[16]E-mail to author from David Messer, First Baptist Church, Asheville, N.C., 26 February, 2001.

[17]Letter from Mary Ann Hobbs, First Baptist Church, Clinton, N.C., March 9, 2000.

[18]E-mail to author from Violet Smith, Germanton Baptist Church, Germanton, N.C., 9 February 2001.

[19]Interview with Jim Fowler.

[20]E-mail to author from Jimmie Hughes, Oakmont Baptist Church, Greenville, N.C., 15 February 2001.

[21]E-mail to author from Alison Bailey, Woodhaven Baptist Church, Apex, N.C.

[22]Interview with Ruth Smith.

[23]Interview with Gary McCullough, Konnoak Baptist Church, Winston-Salem, N.C., January 25, 2000.

[24]Letter from Sandy Spaugh, February 1, 2000.

[25]E-mail to author from Jack Glasgow, Zebulon Baptist Church, Zebulon, N.C., 21 February 2001.

[26]E-mail to author from Violet Smith.

[27]E-mail to author from Keith Breedlove, First Baptist Church, Morganton, N.C.

[28]Interview with Eddie Morgan, First Baptist Church, Asheville, N.C., February 19, 2001.

[29]Interview with Jim Everette, First Baptist Church, Wilmington, N.C., February 24, 2001.

[30]Letter from Sandi McCullough, Konnoak Baptist Church, Winston-Salem, N.C., n.d.

[31]Testimony given at Snyder Memorial Baptist Church, October, 2000.

[32]Mother Teresa, quoted in Malcolm Muggeridge, *Something Beautiful for God* (New York: Doubleday, 1977), 53.

[33]Interview with Rusty Long and Sue Byrd, Fayetteville Urban Ministry, Fayetteville, N.C., February 13, 2001.

[34]Interview with Ruth Smith.

[35]Testimony by Nancy Hollings, Snyder Memorial Baptist Church, Fayetteville, N.C., n.d.

[36]Gordon Loux and Ronald E. Wilson, *You Can Be a Point of Light: Volunteering in Your Community* (Portland, Oreg.: Multnomah Press, 1991), 27–28.

Chapter 3: Hands-on Mission Helps Community

[1]David Sinclair, "Hands-on Mission Helps Community," *The Fayetteville Observer-Times*, 20 October 1996, 1A.

[2]Interview with Rusty Long and Sue Byrd, Fayetteville Urban Ministry, Fayetteville, N.C., February 13, 2001.

[3]Interview with Rusty Long.

[4]Interview with Marty Buie, Cumberland County Council on Older Adults, Fayetteville, N.C., February 15, 2001.

[5]Letter to author received from Buford and Jane Robinson, Morganton, N.C., March 19, 2001.

[6]Interview with Jim Everette, Ardmore Baptist Church, Winston-Salem, N.C., February 24, 2001.

[7]E-mail to author from Violet Smith, Germanton Baptist Church, Germanton, N.C., 9 February 2001.

[8]Interview with Greg Miller, Lafayette Baptist Church, Fayetteville, N.C., March 15, 2000.

[9]E-mail to author from Wendy Edwards, Baptist State Convention of North Carolina, 27 March 2001.

[10]E-mail to the author from Jack Glasgow, Zebulon Baptist Church, Zebulon, N.C., 21 February 2001.

[11]Interview with Roger Stancil, city manager, City of Fayetteville, N.C., February 15, 2001.

[12]Testimony by Sue Byrd, Snyder Memorial Baptist Church, Fayetteville, N.C., 1999.

[13]Interview with Rusty Long.

[14]Robert Bell, "Volunteers Pitch In," *The Fayetteville Observer-Times*, 18 October 1998, 1B.

Chapter 4: The Young and the Restless

[1]Kevin Graham Ford, *Jesus for a New Generation* (Downers Grove, Ill.: InterVarsity Press, 1995), 139.

[2]Audiotape by Paul Borthwick, "Motivating Boomers and Busters for Missions," ACMC, n.d.

[3]Gary McIntosh, *Three Generations* (Grand Rapids, Mich.: Revell, 1995), 133–39.

[4]Leonard Sweet, *SoulTsunami* (Grand Rapids, Mich.: Zondervan, 1999), 205.

[5]McIntosh, *Three Generations*, 138.

[6]George Barna, *Baby Busters: The Disillusioned Generation* (Chicago: Northfield Publishing, 1994), 72–74.

[7]Cassity Dale,

[8]Barna, *Baby Busters*, 73.

[9]Ibid., 74.

[10]"Reaching Generation NeXt," accessed Feb. 7, 2001 at http://www.bgct.org/csc/Busters.html.

[11]Robert N. Nash Jr., *An 8–Track Church in a CD World* (Macon, Ga.: Smyth & Helwys, 1997).

[12]Nash, *An 8–Track Church*, 3.

[13]Interview with Al Cadenhead, Providence Baptist Church, Charlotte, N.C., February 19, 2001.

[14]Barna, *Baby Busters*, 81.

[15]McIntosh, *Three Generations*, 145–46.

[16]Paul Mundey, "Doing Church in a Postmodern Land," Fall 1998. http://www.churchoutreach.com/archive/as-3mundey.shtml.

[17]Nash, *An 8–Track Church*, 104.

[18]McIntosh, *Three Generations*, 163.

[19]Sweet, *SoulTsunami*, 195–96,

[20]Jimmie Hughes, "Operation Inasmuch at Oakmont Baptist Church, Greenville, North Carolina," e-mail to the author, February 12, 2001.

[21]Interview with Vicky Perry, Winter Park Baptist Church, Wilmington, N.C., February 24, 2001.

[22]Sweet, *SoulTsunami*, 214.

[23]Ibid., 189.

[24]Ibid., 216.

[25]Ken Baker, "Boomers, Busters, and Missions: Things are different now," http://www.wheaton.edu/bgc/EMIS/archives/boomers.html.

[26]Sweet, *SoulTsunami*, 219.

[27]Interview with Kenneth Rust, First Baptist Church, Lumberton, N.C., February 12, 2001.

[28]Sweet, *SoulTsunami*, 227.

[29]E-mail to author from Lori Massey, Mars Hill, N.C., 14 February 2001.

Chapter 5: Making the Grade

[1]For a thorough analysis of the power of the parable of the good Samaritan to motivate people to care for others, see chapter 6 of Robert Wuthnow's *Acts of Compassion* (Princeton, N.J.: Princeton Univ. Press, 1991).

[2]Philip Yancey, *Reality and the Vision* (Waco, Tex.: Word, 1990), 87.

[3]Not all congregations have used the name Operation Inasmuch. Some other designations for this one-day event are Mission Morganton, Asheville First, Doers of the Word, Mission Possible, and World Changer Day. In referring to some of these events in this book, I have inserted the name Operation Inasmuch in brackets to simplify understanding.

[4]Avery T. Willis Jr., *The Biblical Basis of Missions* (Nashville: Convention Press, 1984), 9–10.

[5]Ibid., 10.

Chapter 6: This Is the Church

[1]Esther Burroughs, *Empowered: Reclaiming the Meaning of Missions Through the Power of the Holy Spirit* (Birmingham, Ala.: Women's Missionary Union, 1990), 44.

[2]Ad in *Leadership* (Summer 1982): 9, cited by Gordon Loux and Ronald E. Wilson, *You Can Be a Point of Light: Volunteering in Your Community* (Portland, Oreg.: Multnomah Press, 1991), 94.

[3]Cited in Tony Campolo, *20 Hot Potatoes Christians Are Afraid To Touch* (Waco, Tex.: Word, 1988), 31.

[4]Loux and Wilson, *Point of Light*, 90–91.

[5]Letter from Jimmie Mitchell, First Baptist Church, Fayetteville, N.C., n.d.

[6]Excerpt from sermon notes taken from a sermon by J. Alfred Smith, circa 1989.

[7]Norman Cousins, *Dr. Schweitzer of Lambaréné* (Westport, Conn.: Greenwood Press, 1973).

Chapter 7: Mobilizing Volunteers

[1]"Personal Stories," 31 December, 2000, http://www.energizeinc.com/reflect/story.html.

[2]"Giving and Volunteering in the United States: Findings from a National Survey," 1999, accessed March 24, 2005 through http://www.independentsector.org.

[3]"Ministry Involvement," Barna Research Online, 6 February 2001, http://216.87.179.136/cgi-bin/PageCategory.asp?CategoryID=28> Barna Web site as of March 2005 is www.barna.org.

[4]Susan K. E. Saxon-Harrold, "America's Religious Congregations: Measuring Their Contribution to Society," *Independent Sector* (November 2000): 6.

[5]Saxon-Harrold, "America's Religious Congregations," 4.

[6]Robert Wuthnow, *Acts of Compassion: Caring for Others and Helping Ourselves* (Princeton: Princeton Univ. Press, 1991), 125–35.

[7]Ibid., 137.

[8]Robert Lupton, cited in Gordon Loux and Ronald E. Wilson, *You Can Be a Point of Light: Volunteering in Your Community* (Portland, Oreg.: Multnomah Press, 1991), 32–33.

[9]Wuthnow, *Acts of Compassion*, 49.

[10]"Giving and Volunteering in the United States."

[11]Information accessed March 24, 2005 from http://www.peacecorps.com/index.cfm?shell=Learn.whatispc.history.decades.

[12]"Giving and Volunteering in the United States (2001)."

[13]Interview with Mary Poole, First Baptist Church, Clinton, N.C., February 7, 2000.

[14]Wuthnow, *Acts of Compassion*, 56.

[15]Dorothea Dix, cited in Loux and Wilson, *You Can Be a Point of Light*, 31–32.

[16]Loux and Wilson, *You Can Be a Point of Light*, 81.

[17]Interview with Terry Childers, First Baptist Church, Marion, N.C., February 21, 2001.

[18]Nancy Sears (Pleasant Grove Baptist Church, Fuquay-Varina, N.C.), "Operation Inasmuch," e-mail to the author, 12 February 2001.

[19]Letter from Stafford Currin, Snyder Memorial Baptist Church, Fayetteville, N.C., n.d.

[20]Wuthnow, *Acts of Compassion*, 87.

[21]Ibid., 86.

[22]Loux and Wilson, *You Can Be a Point of Light*, 56.

[23]Pam Dass and Paul Gorman, *How Can I Help?* (New York: Knopf, 1987), 10, cited in Wuthnow, *Acts of Compassion*, 61.

[24]Edward LeJoly, *Servant of Love* (New York: Harper and Row, 1977), 13, cited in Loux and Wilson, *You Can Be a Point of Light*, 86.

[25]Marlene Wilson, "What Can We Do About It?" on Energize, Inc. Web site, accessed March 24, 2005 at http://www.energizeinc.com/art/ahow.html.

Chapter 8: Plan the Work, Work the Plan

[1]Interview with Kenneth Rust, First Baptist Church, Lumberton, N.C., February 12, 2001.

[2]Interview with Eddie Morgan, First Baptist Church, Asheville, N.C., February 19, 2001.

[3]Interview with Eddie Morgan.

[4]Interview with Al Cadenhead, Providence Baptist Church, Charlotte, N.C., February 19, 2001.

[5]Interview with Fred Schuszler and Barbara Lambert, First Baptist Church, Morganton, N.C., February 20, 2001.

[6]E-mail to author from Van Lankford, Dobson Baptist Church, Dobson, N.C., 13 March 2001.

Chapter 9: Mission Outpost

[1]Edward H. Hammett, *The Gathered and Scattered Church: Equipping Believers for the 21st Century* (Macon: Smyth & Helwys, 1999), 27.

[2]Interview with Mary Jane Baker, March 17, 2001; all the interviews cited in this chapter were conducted with people from St. James Lutheran on March 17, the day of Operation Inasmuch.

[3]Interview with Robin Ramirez.

[4]Interview with Dave Gorman.

[5]Interview with Larry Hilbert.

[6]Interview with Carol Nelson.

[7]Interview with Mariel Runkle.

[8]Interview with Kathy Arle.

[9]Interview with Rev. Louise Hilbert.

[10]Interview with Rev. Hilbert.

[11]Interview with Rev. Hilbert.

[12]Interview with Ryan Johnson.

[13]Interview with unnamed teenager.

[14]Comment from unidentified volunteer.

[15]E-mail to author from Alyson Wood, St. James Lutheran Church.

[16]Note in "The Messenger," a monthly publication of St. James Lutheran Church, volume 17, no. 4, April 2001, 2.

[17]Interview with Rev. Hilbert.

Chapter 10: The Multi-church Experience

[1]This chapter was added in the fall of 2004. It reflects a change in ministry location for the author from Fayetteville, N.C., to Knoxville, Tenn. It also reports some of the experiences of the author in leading his new church to conduct their first Operation Inasmuch and share it with other neighbor congregations in Knoxville.

[2]Interview with Pam Eubanks, September 25, 2004, Knoxville, Tenn.

[3]Interview with Kathy Rosenbalm, September 23, 2004, Knoxville, Tenn.

[4]Interview with Martha Johnson, September 27, 2004, Knoxville, Tenn.

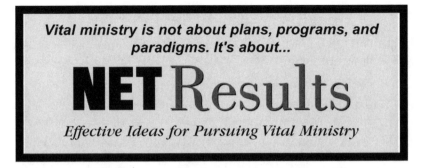

Contents of Resource DVD-ROM

The DVD-ROM includes several resources for promoting and organizing an Operation Inasmuch in your church. The DVD-ROM has two folders:

Video Folder (DVD player required to view video)

This nine-minute video shows scenes from an actual Operation Inasmuch. (There is no sound on the video until the Inasmuch scripture comes onscreen.)

"The Basin and the Towel" written by Michael Card, © Birdwing Music. Michael Card appears courtesy of Sparrow Records. The song (product #SPD1421) originally recorded on *Poeima* (P) Sparrow Records (admin. EMI Christian Music Group).

Support Materials Folder (software required noted)

> OIAM logo
> PowerPoint Presentation *(MS PowerPoint)*
> Project/Volunteer Master List *(MS Excel)*
> Consent Form (Youth Release Form) *(MS Word)*
> Name Tags *(MS Word)*
> Sign-up Forms *(MS Word)*
> Letter to Project Leaders *(MS Word)*
> Final Reminder to Project Leaders *(MS PowerPoint)*
> Lunch Reminder *(MS PowerPoint)*
> Song: "In His Name," used by permission of Rita B. Carroll. All rights reserved. *(Acrobat Reader)*
> Song: "I Worship You," used by permission of Vickie W. Willis, Scott Willis, and Jon E. Conley. All rights reserved. (Audio player for audio tracks, *MS Word* for chord chart)

PC users

To play video: Operation Inasmuch screen may automatically appear when you insert the DVD into the computer. If so, click on Play Video. If not, go to My Computer and double-click on the DVD drive, then click Play Video. *To access the support materials:* Go to My Computer, right-click on the DVD drive, click on Open, and double-click on the Support Materials folder.

Mac users

To play a video: Open your DVD player software and hit play (or hit play under the Control menu). To escape the DVD player, move your cursor to top of screen, go to File and then Quit. *To access the support materials:* Double-click on the DVD drive icon on your desktop and double-click on the Support Materials folder.